Building a Modern Datacenter in the Azure Cloud

Mini-Book Technology Series – Book 4

Chris Amaris, MCITP, CISSP
Marcus Clayton, MCSA, MCSE
Rand Morimoto, Ph.D., MCSE

DEDICATION

I dedicate this book Sophia and our 5 children, Michelle, Megan, Zoe, Zachary, and Ian - Chris Amaris

I dedicate this book to Vicki, thanks for supporting me on this journey; and to my parents George and Tracey, thanks for sending me to college, you're in my book, we're even - Marcus Clayton

I dedicate this book to my peers on the Microsoft IPAC and those who lead and make the PAC meetings valuable, thank you! - Rand Morimoto

ACKNOWLEDGMENTS

Thank you to all of our clients whom we've worked with over the past several years as we've migrated their datacenters to Microsoft's Azure cloud. What works best always starts with early adopters and strategic implementers, and we've been fortunate to have many organizations that have leveraged the latest technologies to formulate a definitive process of what works and what doesn't. The results of these efforts is what has been provided in the pages of this book.

TABLE OF CONTENTS

INTRODUCTION

As organizations shift their I.T. operations to run in a hosted cloud environment, the biggest mistake that is made is building their modern cloud environment to mirror exactly how their on-premise datacenters were architected 20-years ago. Old fashioned datacenters were constrained by the limitations of physical hardware, overpowered because hardware depreciation schedules required equipment to last at least 3-5 years, and were architected to be overly complicated because the failure of a component could take days to acquire a replacement part. Organizations that build their cloud environment exactly the same have completely missed the point about how additional capacity can be purchased with a click of a button, and that excess capacity can be eliminated with the running of a one line script.

This mini-book covers new models of cloud-based application and systems architecture that leverages the inherent agility and elasticity of the cloud, providing real world examples of automation scripts and operational best practice processes.

1 DATACENTERS OF THE PAST, ARE DATACENTERS OF THE PAST

Most on-premise datacenters are based on a 20+ year old architecture concept where servers and storage capacity were limited, hardware was unreliable, and site connectivity was slow. As organizations shifted from 32-bit hardware to 64-bit hardware, physical servers to virtual machines, and point to point 1Mbps T1 network connections to fully meshed 10Gbps networks, the general architecture didn't evolve as drastically as the capability of the underlying technology.

As organizations shift from their on-premise datacenters to newer cloud-based models, this has become the prime opportunity for datacenter architects to rethink their infrastructure models to leverage current technologies, and not simply transition decades old concepts and constructs into much more robust cloud environments.

64-bit as an Exponential Leap in Performance

A decade ago, a major improvement in technology slipped its way into our datacenters, but occurred at a time when so many other things were going on that only recently have organizations thought about the impact 64-bit computing had in our day to day operations. The big thing most organizations remember of the time is the shift from physical server systems to server virtualization, effectively the rise of VMware that allowed organizations to run many servers on a single hardware system.

But virtualization would have never happened if it weren't for 64-bit computing. With 32-bit computing, a host's operating system was limited to 4-gigabytes of memory, barely enough to run one instance of a server application, let alone try to squeeze two or more servers to run on the same hardware. With 64-bit hardware and operating systems, servers were being outfitted with 16gb, 32gb, 64gb of memory allowing for one server to run 4, 8, 12 virtual server instances on a single piece of hardware.

While over the past decade organizations have benefited from virtualizing their server instances and running more applications on fewer hardware systems, what most organizations failed to do was account for the fact that applications running on 64-bit systems instead of 32-bit systems could also handle a higher density of users, requiring fewer virtual instances for applications.

Active Directory (AD) domain controllers are probably the most visible server instances that haven't adjusted to address the capacity afforded by 64-bit runtimes. Microsoft Exchange Server email systems used to have a rule of thumb of 1 domain controller for every 4 email servers under a 32-bit Active Directory configuration, but scaled that to 1 domain controller for every 8 email servers under a 64-bit Active Directory configuration. Yet it is very common to see organizations running AD on 64-bit platforms, while holding on to the 4:1 ratio as if they were still running in the 32-bit era.

Even Exchange Servers themselves that organizations used to have one email server for every 500-1000 mailboxes back in the old Exchange v5.5, 32-bit environment days could easily run 20,000-50,000 mailboxes on a single 64-bit Exchange 2016 server today, yet the density and distribution hasn't made its way to being updated in server architecture with organizations.

Organizations can usually eliminate at least 50% of their servers from the environment if they truly scaled the servers to what they actually need given the current hardware capabilities of systems.

64-bit Opened the Door for Larger Databases

The 64-bit operating system and applications also increased the storage capacity in databases, which were previously limited to 16gb per database for most 32-bit based database systems. The 16gb database limit was extended to 100gb-200gb sizes on 32-bit systems, but these days with 64-bit operating systems and applications, databases can be 100x or more in size, yet many organizations still base their database size limits to configuration standards appropriate for older 32-bit configurations rather than current best practices.

Database sizes should not be based on a perceived notion that there's an operating system limitation on today's 64-bit platforms. In fact, they don't even need to be chunked up based on active and inactive data given the current Stretched DB technologies.

Much of the reasoning for size limitations no longer apply, and a reassessment of an organizations application architecture as they shifts to a cloud-based model can optimize the configuration of servers and systems in the new model. Simply moving over archaic and inefficient designs do not allow an organization to take advantage of the advancements made in the last few years.

Reliable Meshed Networks Require Less Redundancy

When network connections were point to point, with intermittent network and site failures, having a "replica" of authentication servers, application servers, databases in each site was the best practice. When a site or connection failed a decade ago, organizations wanted a local replica so that employees could continue working.

The need for overly complex redundancy in each site was no longer a requirement as networks became more reliable, servers and storage systems became more redundant, and networks became fully meshed with high speed connectivity to other sites. Even with these advancements, it is still common to see organizations with a domain controller in each site (many times 2 domain controllers in each site), a fileserver in each location replicated with other servers in the same location plus made redundant to another site "just in case".

This redundancy is justified by many I.T. professionals stating that if there is a site failure, and a local domain controller or file server is not present, employees wouldn't be able to get their work done. This is a common concern and design approach from network administrators, who continue to build connectivity without considering their cloud presence. For an organization whose email system is cloud-based, when their internet connection fails, users are not receiving email, so having a local fileserver likely won't make a difference from a productivity standpoint.

Replicas and Digital Backups Recover Faster

Another reason for organizations to limit the size of databases, and thus their need for way more servers than they truly need was based on the backup and restoral times it took to manage large databases. Many best practices a decade ago was to limit systems to 100gb-250gb in size so that the systems can be backed up and restored to tape in a reasonable timeframe. These days, tape is not (and should not) be the method of backup and recovery. While digital backup and recovery solutions may still exist in organizations, they should be used for archival purposes where a 2, 3, or even a 5-day restoral time for compliance recovery purposes is adequate.

Actual high availability and real time disaster recovery (DR) solutions should involve the replication of data between servers and/or sites with failover mechanisms that can recover a system within minutes. These technologies exist, should be utilized by enterprises in their transition to the cloud, and thus allowing the size of databases and server utilization to expand. As a result, an organization can reduce the footprint and number of servers managed in their environment.

More Reliable Components Minimizes the Layers of Redundancy Required

Over the past couple decades, server systems, storage, and networking components have all become more reliable. Daily hard drive replacement and weekly memory chip swap-outs are a thing of the past. Systems purchased these days have redundant power supplies, with redundant memory chips, 4-5 layers of redundant storage, multi-path meshed networking technologies and do not require 3-4 levels of additional redundancy. Yet most enterprise architectures have 2-3 servers in a primary datacenter and 1-2 replicas in a disaster recovery datacenter, when 1 is all that is needed to run the application.

Most global scale cloud providers don't buy $50,000 servers, they implement cheap $500 servers, put in 2-3 way redundancy in a site, and 2-3 way redundancy across sites, so for $5,000 they have 9-ways of redundancy compared to a single $50,000 server that is still a single point of failure. When the organization pays for 99.98% uptime redundancy on a cloud-based server instance or service, the organization has to take in account whether it needs 2-3 replicas of those types of instances in a datacenter, or whether they may simply buy the single node capacity they need, add a geo-redundant replica in another datacenter for site resiliency, and eliminate the cost and complexity of managing redundancy on top of redundancy in the new cloud-based architecture

New Environment, New Design

It is these changes in design and architecture that organizations need to rethink and build their new cloud-based environment around what is possible today, instead of merely bringing forward legacy designs based on 10 and 20 year old models, no longer applicable in this day and age. The next three chapters of this book go through new models for architecture that'll help in the planning and development of more modern and efficient methods of environment implementation.

2 THE ECONOMIC BURDEN OF THE LEGACY DATACENTER

Besides just the technical advances that datacenter architecture failed to keep in step as technology performance, reliability, and scalability progressed, most organizations running their own datacenters are still burdened by the fundamental constraints of amortization and depreciation schedules of capital purchases.

The Three to Five Year Depreciation Schedule

Tax laws typically limit organizations from expensing capital purchases of technology equipment to a minimum of 3-years, and many times 5-7 years. Whether the technology is even viable in 5-years, organizations have been stuck with the equipment. Many organizations have shifted to a leasing structure where they can lease their datacenter hardware for 2-3 years, thus shifting from a capital purchase with a 5-7 year depreciation schedule, to a 2-3 year schedule that gets expensed each month.

However, organizations with their own datacenters are still "stuck" with hardware for 2, 3, or 5+ years whether the equipment (hardware and software) is appropriately sized, scaled, or meet the needs of the organization.

Overbuy Capacity to Last Five Years

The result of being "stuck" with hardware and software for several years is that organizations have developed a habit of overbuying capacity. If you only need capacity for 1,000 users, but the company is expected to grow 2-3 times in the next 5-years, then the organization would buy capacity to support 2,000-3,000 users so that their systems will support the projected demands the organization may have during the depreciated life of the equipment.

Beyond just overbuying capacity to support the potential growth in the number of employees, organizations have realized that their storage demands grow exponentially, so if the organization grows 20TB a year and the storage system is to last 5-years, the organization would purchase 100+TB of storage, again not using the storage for a few years, but just having the storage to meet the potential future needs of the organization.

Overbuy Capacity for Redundancy

In addition to overbuying capacity for actively used systems, organizations then bought even more capacity for redundancy and disaster recovery. For redundancy, if the organization only needed 1 system (that was to last 5-years), the organization would buy 2-3 systems (similarly over configured to last 5-years) in case the primary system failed. Upon failover, the redundant (overly sized) system had to have equivalent capacity to handle the load.

That 1 system the organization turned in to 2-3 systems, and those 2-3 systems were then replicated to a disaster recovery datacenter so that if the primary site failed, the DR site could take up the load. Following the same design pattern, the failover site couldn't just have 1 system properly sized for what the organization actually needed, that failover center also had to be sized to support the 5+ year potential capacity requirement, and not just 1 failover system but 2-3 just in case the failover site had to run for several weeks.

For every 1 system an organization actually needed, organizations had 5-10 times the capacity actually required, all because the tax depreciation schedules forced organizations into a buying model that met tax laws, not operational demand models.

Overbuy for Hardware Consistency and Availability

In addition to buying excess capacity to account for getting "stuck" with hardware for 5-years and the need to overbuy capacity in event of equipment failure, organizations have also overbought capacity because hardware makes and models go obsolete after 12-24 months. If the organization is setting up a clustered environment that really only needed 2 nodes, if one of those systems failed 2-years down the line, the organization would likely not be able to buy an identical system and configuration needed to replace the node. Many replicated technologies required similar if not identical systems for failover that included the same make and model of network adapter, video adapter, storage controller, and the like, and thus a 2-node cluster ended up being a 4-node cluster just to maintain similar hardware during the 3-5 year depreciation schedule forced model.

Even if the same make and model of equipment were to be available 2 or 3 years later, product acquisition time of generating a purchase order and the shipping of the equipment to the site and the time to setup and configure the system forced organizations again to pre-buy, configure, and run excess capacity just because it could take 2-4 weeks to get an order placed and replacement hardware delivered and setup.

Managing the Capacity

While high performance 64-bit technology could likely allow an organization to run much of their core applications on just 5-10 servers TOTAL in the organization, the aforementioned over purchase of capacity resulted in organizations ending up with 2-3 redundant datacenters with 30-50 servers each, and a footprint of 100-200 host servers running hundreds of overly redundant and over capacity configured systems.

With this sprawl of servers, storage, redundant systems, and sites, organizations have a dire need to monitor, secure, and manage that capacity. Entire environments of management systems have been added to maintain the systems. Many organizations have just as many monitoring, management, and security systems as they have actual operational systems, doubling the footprint of the organization. These management systems usually require just as many resources to run, adding to the overall operational overhead of the enterprise.

1% Need / 99% Overhead

As covered in the book "Application and Datacenter Modernization" (Morimoto/Amaris, 2016, ISBN 978-1537664996), organizations have an application and data demand of 1%, with 99% of their I.T. operations spent on the overhead associated to this overcapacity of servers and systems to account for the 3-5 year tax depreciation schedule, anticipated organization growth, redundancy to overcompensate for the need for identical replica systems, overcapacity to handle failover as well as site disaster recovery, and all of the systems needed to monitor, manage, and maintain this sprawl of systems.

For those who cannot believe this 1% rule is accurate, look at the average utilization of a core application server over a 14-day period, and the realization that a server is running at likely 3%-5% utilization means just that 1 system has 95+% excess capacity. Then simply count the number of load balanced and clustered nodes for that system, and the number of sites and backups that system has, and then the number of management systems used to monitor and manage that system, and one can easily take a 3%-5% utilized system and realize the actual usage is 2%, 1%, or less than 1%.

3 THE INHERENT BENEFITS OF THE PUBLIC CLOUD

Cloud computing inherently is bought and consumed as needed. Organizations may buy a "little" excess capacity to account for a 3% or 5% blip in demand, but not the 99% excess capacity in today's traditional datacenter.

Buying Compute and Storage Capacity as Needed

Virtual machine servers in the cloud can be sized based on what the organization needs today with a small amount of overhead (~5%) . If the organization needs more capacity, it can quickly and easily spin up resources in a matter of minutes, that'll be highlighted in Chapter 9 "Building Cloud Infrastructure on Demand" of this book on specific real world scripts and processes to add capacity on demand.

Instead of running server capacity at 3%-5%, an organization can buy and run cloud server systems at 70% or even 90%, pushing the limits of the system for better overall utilization.

Storage in the cloud is only paid for as used, there's no need to pre-purchase storage capacity. If the organization needs more storage, simply consume the storage and pay for the amount in use (pay-as-you-go).

Leveraging Cloud Uptime

When capacity is purchased in the cloud, it comes with a guaranteed uptime on the services, whether that's 99.97% or some variation. The organization does not necessarily need to then buy 2 or 3 more systems for redundancy unless they are actually needed for immediate capacity demand.

Many organizations may conservatively choose to buy a second system even if they may not need it just as a safety net until such time the organization is comfortable that their cloud provider can truly provide the uptime committed. The recommendation is to set a timeline on how long the organization will allow for this excess "comfort capacity," whether that's 6 months or a year, and then eliminate that excess capacity thereafter.

Additionally, the organization may selectively choose a handful of truly mission critical business applications to overbuy a "little" excess capacity, but for the other 70%-80% of the applications, to skinny down those configurations to just what the organization requires.

Cloud-based Geo-Redundancy

When excess capacity for redundancy is purchased, rather than buying excess capacity in the same datacenter, the organization should purchase the redundancy capacity in a different geo-location. This will provide the organization that "extra safety net" that it wants with its mission critical application, as well as provide a point of geo-redundancy that can benefit the organization in true application disaster recovery.

By default, major cloud providers typically offer within-continent redundancy as part of their 99.97% uptime commitments, so the multi-continent redundancy truly provides a replication state for better reliability. There is no need for organizations to build, manage, and maintain an excess amount of geo and global high availability and disaster recovery with cloud services. Buy what you need, when you need it!

Eliminate the Cost of Obsolescence

Unlike the 3-5 year tax depreciation schedule restricted model, with cloud computing, an organization can upgrade their systems to newer configurations at any point in time. If the organization wants 2 more core processors, the organization can simply buy 2 more core processors to add to their configuration. If the organization wants to upgrade to a 7th, 8th, or

9th generation processor technology, they can purchase that technology after 2-years, 2-months, or 2-weeks. The organization isn't "stuck" with what they start off using. The mindset has to be reset that the acquisition of technology is based solely on what the organization absolutely needs right now, and then buy and upgrade if and when more employees are hired, demands increase, or new technologies are needed to run a particular software upgrade.

Some of the technologies organizations look to for future upgrades include next generation solid state storage, 128-bit compute technology, graphical acceleration processors, and the like. As these technologies are needed for the organization's applications, the technologies can be acquired on demand.

Decreasing Compute and Storage Costs as Managed

As much as the focus of this chapter has been to buy additional capacity as an organization's demands grow, what is also important in the optimization of cloud computing is the ability to decrease capacity when the demand is not needed. If the organization decreases the number of employees it has due to downsizing, maybe seasonal decreases, potentially even the application demand decreases, the organization should eliminate capacity. Cloud computing is paid for by the allocation of resources. Deallocate and stop paying for capacity if it is not needed.

The elimination of capacity isn't just decreasing the number of core processors allocated, but can also be eliminated by deleting (or archiving and removing) outdated data. If the organization only needs to keep data for 7-years, start deleting old data. While it initially might not be a lot of data removed, as organizations have begun to exponentially store data in the past 3-4 years, that 7-year deletion will be significant in 3-4 years from now, so start the process now.

Unlike traditional datacenter purchases where you bought it and have to keep it whether you use it or not, cloud allows organizations to buy and spend less based on their needs.

4 ARCHITECTING THE CLOUD-BASED DATACENTER

For technology architects building a cloud environment, as has been the focus of this book, the approach isn't to take archaic datacenter, application, and hardware constraints and build a new cloud-based datacenter the same way. The new design for the cloud-based datacenter is to fully leverage the strengths and solutions provided by the cloud service providers.

Assessing Applications, not Servers

The first step for cloud architects is to look at what employees do, the applications they use, and how they do their jobs. This reassessment process enables the architect to determine employee usage requirements, how technology fits into the day to day tasks of the employees, and provides the architect the ability to plan and implement a cloud model that meets the current needs of the organizations.

Employees typically communicate over email and instant messaging, store and access files, and run business applications that control manufacturing, track sales, or the like. As digital technologies have expanded, many organizations find employees do not use "phone systems" as much as they used to, or the use of paper-based content has diminished. Many organizations have found they can eliminate 50-70% of their phone lines and drastically decrease telephony costs because employees simply don't use their office phones anymore.

And unlike in the past where you bought a phone system to support all employees, disconnecting 50% of the users didn't necessarily decrease costs since the hardware was purchased on a 5-year depreciation schedule. Today when services are purchased "per user, per month", the elimination of user configurations can immediately decrease costs. When the administrator goes to the licensing portal and un-checks a license box, the incurring cost for those users are eliminated. Granted some licenses are based on a 1-year or 3-year license commitment, however surprisingly to many I.T. professionals, those 3-year lock in pricing are mostly 1-year commitment schedules, and many vendors have truly gone to a month by month schedule. This means if you don't need it, disable it, and don't make the assumption that you won't save the company money. In the cloud model, non-use is non-use, disable and start the process of cleaning up as you go.

Many organizations have multiple technologies with overlapping functionality that the organization can choose to collapse and minimize the technological spend on redundant solutions. As much as "some" users may be active users of a solution, a cost analysis can help management make the decision to eliminate lightly used systems. While it may be unpopular to the handful of users that are inconvenienced by the elimination of the solution, removing the decision from the hands of I.T. and getting the agreement of the Chief Financial Officer of the organization to determine whether it is worthwhile for the organization to continue to invest in a lightly used application, or simply make the decision to sunset the application over time. And if the application will be eliminated, that application may reside onsite for a 6, 12, or 18 month ramp down period and not be included in the migration to the cloud.

By looking at the applications and the business uses by employees, the focus of the modern datacenter is to fulfill employee services, not mirror server solutions to continue the operation, management, and support of every product and solution ever used by the organization forever.

Assessing User Access Locations and Density

An assessment of user access locations and the density of use in locations helps the cloud architect determine the design and distribution of cloud services for the enterprise. For organizations that used to be heavily dependent on "corporate sites" and have since shifted to a more mobile workforce, rethinking whether having a high speed internet connection from every site is necessary.

The movement to a cloud-based environment doesn't immediately require the organization to increase its internet connection capacity, in fact for many organizations whose users are predominantly mobile users, their connection from their mobile devices to the cloud service that never passes through the enterprise datacenter means the datacenter connection doesn't need to be as robust nor redundant.

When applications were distributed across multiple enterprise datacenter sites, the need to have high speed site to site connectivity is diminished as users now only need to access their data in a cloud service. Many organizations find site to site connectivity to be virtually eliminated, along with all of the internetworking that was implemented over the years to facilitate a very robust site-focused model.

Identity at the Root of information Systems

An important component for organizations in the new model of enterprise computing is knowing WHO is logging on to ensure that the individual accessing enterprise resources is indeed the person that the organizations believes to be the one logging in. This identity model extends the where and what from the last section, to include "who" needs access to what information from where.

In addition to having an identity system that ensures the integrity of the access of individuals, organizations will want to confirm they have multi-factor authentication systems and security access controls that meet the current standards in enterprises. Rather than depending just on a simple logon and password, multi-factor authentication systems can tie to mobile phones, smartcards, or other devices that challenge the user upon logon, and minimize the risk caused by simple logon and password authentication systems.

Security access controls, specifically around role-based security and "just enough security" models isolate security so that an individual only has access to what they need. The big change is for the administrators of the network themselves, who are now the target of security attacks. Network administrators have for years given themselves full access to install, configure, backup, and maintain everything in the network. Security attackers know that, and rather than attacking the network, they are phishing and looking to compromise the administrators. A simple breach of an administrator's logon gives the attacker full access to everything.

By defining roles and minimizing who has access to what information may be seem inconvenient, when the administrator no longer has to back up the system at night, installs and configures systems, and no longer directly manages operational services, many of the traditional permissions can be eliminated from the administrator's day to day account.

As we'll get into the automation process of server builds and configurations, with scripted processes taking over the mundane tasks, the administrator themselves no longer have direct responsibility to create systems, this is where the roles of security are most visibility changed.

Moving Applications to "As a Service"

As organizations leverage cloud-based technologies, the decision is whether to "move" applications as virtual machines from an on-premise datacenter to a cloud-based virtual machine, or move the application as a service. A good example of technologies proven to be successful in the cloud as a service are email systems, file sharing systems, document collaboration systems, and telephony.

These services are commodity, email is for the most part identical for all organizations that open, read, print, create, and send email messages. File sharing is the same across organizations of opening, saving, storing, and printing files. There's very little uniqueness about these functions between organizations, and thus the applications can easily be moved to a service and eliminate the need for the organization to build, manage, maintain, and support server systems for these applications.

Rewriting Applications "As a Service"

For some applications that have customization specific to an enterprise, those applications can either be moved as a monolithic virtual machine to a cloud-based virtual machine instance, or in many cases the application can be rewritten and hosted as a service. This is commonly done as Platform as a Service (PaaS) application migrations where just a few modifications to an application are required to move and upload to a cloud service to run under a cloud-based PaaS model.

Some organizations may hesitate at the time and effort it'll take to rewrite an application to have it run in a PaaS-based model, however even if it takes 2-3 months to rewrite an application, that can save months and years of ongoing maintenance and management effort of the older legacy-based environment. And as many organizations have found, the rewrite of many applications isn't 2-3 months, but many times 2-3 hours of code revisions, so the time and effort spent to assess applications pays off in the long run.

This elimination of frontend servers, backend servers, load balances, clustered databases, backup, maintenance and management of systems can significantly decrease the operational efforts of an organization.

Sizing Remaining Server-based Applications

For what is left in applications that haven't been targeted and/or already migrated to the cloud as Software as a Service or Platform as a Service models, the next step is to assess the application's true needs to run as an Infrastructure as a Service cloud-hosted virtual machine model. Remembering not to simply take the current (over-spec'd) server configuration and mirror that for the cloud configuration, but to size the applications (+5%) to meet the current needs of the organization.

There is no need to over build capacity, you can always buy more capacity later that can be quickly and simply added as needed. There are a handful of tools that simplify the capacity assessment process, tools from companies like BitTitan and Cloudamize among others run on servers for a couple weeks and then provides a report that notes the actual usage of capacity and demand on servers over the period of time.

Buy Redundancy and Resiliency As a Service

As the organization shifts applications to a cloud-hosted environment, they should also consider utilizing cloud-based redundancy and "resiliency as a service". Most cloud hosting providers offer geo-redundancy at an incremental cost, where the addition of 10%-15% of the cost of running the primary system increases the guaranteed uptime from say 99.9% uptime to 99.97% uptime through some type of datacenter or geo-redundancy service. Effectively don't build redundancy as additional virtual machine instances if you can pay for it as a service.

Redesign Backup as an Archive Not for Redundancy

With guaranteed SLA of 99.95% or 99.99%, traditional "backups" are no longer used for disaster recovery. Organizations are not looking to restore a server from a backup within a few hours, rather backups these days are truly for archival restoral purposes. If an organization wants to recovery information that was purged off their primary systems 2-years ago yet wants data from 5-years ago, a tape backup could be used for recovery. However, the expectation for the recovery of old (2+ year, 5+ year) data is that the information can be recovered within a "few days". As such, the focus of backups are now for historical archiving purposes, not intended for redundancy of systems.

5 CLOUD ARCHITECTURE (A REAL WORLD SCENARIO)

While organizations are different in many ways in what they do, whether they manufacture products, provide professional services, provide healthcare services, are an educational institution, provide research and development services, run a government institution, or the like, at the end of the day, most organizations are similar in how they leverage technology. Employees communicate with one another or with people outside of their organization. Employees perform centralized tasks and/or they perform specialized tasks. Technology is used to structure mundane tasks that help employees reach a goal, fulfill some type of function, and manage some type of functional service.

Identity – Knowing Who is Accessing What

Organizations typically use Microsoft Active Directory as a primary identifier, not that other centralized identity solutions don't exist (ie: Okta, Ping, OneLogin), but Active Directory is the foundation of most organization's identify, and thus all applications connect to and support Active Directory. Active Directory has been a requirement to access Microsoft-centric applications like Exchange email, SharePoint file storage, System Center management systems.

With the integration to cloud services, Microsoft came out with Azure Active Directory (AAD) that extends the traditional on-premise Active

Directory to cloud resources like Microsoft's Office 365, Azure, and Intune services. Azure Active Directory extends identity services like password reset, group security, role-based services, user creation, and account removal to hybrid identity models. Organizations can onboard and eliminate users, and ultimately enable and disable access based on these resource management services which is all part of the enterprise cloud architecture of identity systems.

Email, File sharing, Web Conferencing, and Telephony

Basic business productivity services like email, file sharing, web conferencing, and telephony are part of Microsoft's Office 365 cloud services and has become the enterprise standard. Microsoft provides the latest versions of Outlook, Skype, OneDrive, and Cloud PBX that supports all industry standard endpoint devices like Windows, Apple Mac, iPhones, iPads, and Android systems.

As organizations look to architect their basic business productivity services, shifting to something like Office 365 as a service includes the redundancy, security, disaster recovery, archiving, and eDiscovery that makes up dozens of services I.T. has had to build, manage, and maintain on their own. These comprehensive SaaS-based services make it cheaper and easier for enterprises to leverage critical business services easier than they can do themselves.

Dev and Test in the Cloud

When datacenters were on-premise, organizations built their entire application development systems and their environmental test systems on-premise in mirrored datacenter configurations. With Dev and Test in the cloud, organizations have a choice whether to buy and build racks of servers for these Dev and Test resources, or to leverage the cloud for these services.

Much of the Dev and Test operational build-outs over the past couple years have been leveraging the cloud more than on-premise build-outs primarily because the ability for organizations to scale up in the cloud, and scale down in the cloud without the time and cost of doing the same effort on-premise. Rather than being limited to a fixed number of servers and resources on-premise, organizations can build 1, 10, 100, 1000, 10000 systems in the cloud in minutes, use the resources for an hour, day, week, or month and then completely shut down and stop using the resources and only pay for the number of resources used during a limited timeframe.

Cloud Hoster Diversification

For organizations that are nervous about putting "all their eggs in one basket" with a single vendor or cloud hosted provider, a simple solution to that is to architect a replication and redundancy across cloud providers. For applications that are typically running as an Infrastructure as a Service host virtual machine, the application instances can typically be replicated from server to server, and site to site. A good example of this would be something like Microsoft's SQL Server where Always-On Availability Groups can span SQL databases across datacenters and sites, including replicating between Amazon Web Services and Microsoft Azure.

For Platform as a Service, or cloud application services native to the hosted provider, the replication between providers gets more complicated as you cannot easily replicate a PaaS-based Web application running on Amazon Web Services to a PaaS-based Web instance running in a Microsoft Azure datacenter. This is where Microsoft's Azure Stack has completely changed the way hosted applications and services can be made redundant across providers.

Microsoft's Azure Stack is a common operating platform where "as a service" instances of Web, database, identity, name services and the like run in a defined manner. Azure Stack systems are based on Microsoft's Azure public cloud model, yet can run in 3rd party hoster datacenters as well as on-premise in an organization's own private cloud datacenter. With the same underlying platform, organizations can replicate and triangulate core cloud services across datacenters.

The Cost of Redundancy and Resiliency

I.T. has gotten so focused on redundancy and resiliency "at any cost", organizations have lost sight of the actual cost of redundancy. If the email system is down, organizations feel they need to have an immediate replica of the email system to prevent downtime of emails. But for telephone services, if the phone system is down, does the organization have a completely separate phone system "just in case"? People justify that the phone company was reliable so you didn't need a secondary phone system, however email systems aren't as reliable as phone systems since email servers crash and require redundancy.

However as technology has evolved, and hosted providers of email are just as reliable as the Phone Company was years ago, does this need for redundancy still stand true? When the power goes out in a building, does the organization have a spare (idle) building that employees can shift to in the event of the power outage? Redundancy has a cost to it, and organizations need to assess that cost to determine if they really need to invest in that expense given the reliability of services these days has drastically improved.

This is a major shift in thinking for the architecture of a cloud environment, where "things have changed" and thus a backup of the hosted cloud provider that is operating at 99.97% uptime may not need an individual organization to create a redundant system of the already reliable and dependable service of the cloud provider. If the email system retains mail based on the policies set by the organization to keep emails for 7-years, or 10-years, does the organization need yet another method of backing up emails to provide copies of content 7 or 10-years from now, or just depend on the service level agreement legally contracted with the cloud provider.

Architects of cloud services have a number of new things to think about, plan, design, and build into their models that are very different from what has traditionally been done in the past 5, 10, 20 years.

6 DESIGNING HYBRID IDENTITY

Identity is a key service for organizations to securely provide users authentication and access to applications and services. Since many organizations use Microsoft Active Directory on premise, there are many options for designing a hybrid identity solution around Microsoft AD and Azure Active Directory. Organizations need to decide on the version of Azure Active Directory, if and how to synchronize for single sign-on capabilities, how to provide identity to cloud hosted applications, how to provide domain services to Infrastructure-as-a-Service (IaaS) workloads in Azure, and how to ensure high availability and disaster recovery.

Azure AD

Azure Active Directory (AAD) is multi-tenant cloud based directory and identity management service provided by Microsoft. This is the directory used for the Office 365 SaaS application, to administer Azure services, and to provide single sign-on to a wide variety of applications. Azure AD identity is essential to any organizations on-ramp to Azure and the cloud.

There are different versions of Azure AD, which provide different level of directory features depending on the organization needs. The versions are:

• Azure AD Basic – This provides directory features, single sign-on (SSO), self-service cloud password reset, on-premise

synchronization, and security reporting. This version is best for smaller organizations with an all-in-the-cloud deployment model.
- Azure AD Premium P1 – This provides the same features as Basic, but includes multi-factor authentication, self-service group management, dynamic groups, self-service password reset with on-premise write-back, and health monitoring for on-premise synchronization. The Premium P1 version is best for medium sized organizations with more complex identity management and security needs.
- Azure AD Premium P2 – This provides all the features of Premium P1, but adds advanced security protections with Identity Protection and Privileged Identity Management which provide identity and access monitoring with machine learning. The Premium P2 is the best for medium or large organization where directory and authentication security is important.

It is important to evaluate and select the appropriate version of Azure Active Directory to meet the requirements.

On Premise AD Synchronization for Single Sign-On

However, most organizations will have a Microsoft Windows Server Active Directory Domain Services (AD DS) running on-premise to support their identity, servers, workstations, and applications. This means that the users identity and passwords will most likely preexist and be used by on-premise applications and services, so it is important to provide seamless integration between the on-premise AD DS and the cloud based Azure AD to allow for sign sign-on (SSO).

Microsoft provides the Azure AD Connect tool, which will synchronize AD DS and Azure AD including users, contacts, groups, and passwords. This provides for a common identity and authentication for users to access on-premise resources and applications, SaaS applications such as Office 365, and Azure resources such as web services, IaaS, and PaaS.

Active Directory Domain Services Domain Controller in Azure

Sometimes, an organization will need to host an instance of their on-premise Active Directory DS in the Azure cloud. This could be to:

- Support Isolated Dev-Test Replicas.
- Provide Full Active Directory Services such as Group Policy.
- Support traditional directory-aware applications.

This requires configuring a stretched data center with connectivity to the on-premise network, creating a virtual machine in Azure IaaS, and configuring the virtual machine as a domain controller for the AD DS.

Azure Active Directory Domain Services

Alternatively, to deploying an AD DS domain controller in Azure, Azure provides Azure Active Directory Domain Services. For Azure IaaS virtual machines, Azure AD Domain Services allows organizations to join the virtual machines to the Azure AD without the need for an AD DS domain controller. This is an important option to support traditional directory aware applications in the cloud.

Fault Tolerance and Disaster Recovery

For hybrid configurations, the Azure AD Connect component will be critical for object and password synchronization. Losing the AD Connect functions can result in negative impacts to the users and loss of productivity due to mismatched passwords, to delays in on-boarding users, and even to security breaches if security changes are not replicated between directories. For example, if the AD Connect is offline and a terminated user is disabled in the on-premise AD DS, that change will not be replicated to Azure AD and the terminated user could potentially continue to use cloud services.

There are a variety of design options to provide fault tolerance to the Azure AD Connect service. These can include:

- Hosting Azure AD Connect in Azure – As discussed in "Chapter 3: The Inherent Benefits of the Public Cloud", Azure IaaS is a highly available environment and hosting the AD Connect server there will provide a high degree of fault tolerance, leveraging the native Azure cloud advantages and insulating the service from local on-premise outages such as power failures.
- Azure IaaS Virtual Machine Backup – Using the Operations Management Suite (OMS) IaaS Backup service will provide 1 hour recovery time for the Azure AD Connect server, giving a rapid recovery in the event of a failure and even recovery in the event of a regional failure.
- Staging Mode Standby Server – Additional Azure AD Connect servers can be deployed and configured in Staging Mode. It will receive all the same changes as the Primary Server and so is current, but will not export those changes to Azure AD. In the event of a failure of the Primary Azure AD Connect Server, a Staging Server can be switched to be the Primary Server.

Any organization relying on a hybrid identity needs to have a well-thought out fault tolerance and disaster recovery plan.

Hybrid Identity Small Scenario

For a small organization with a cloud-first strategy and a highly mobile workforce, using Azure SaaS applications such as Office 365 for all its needs and no on-premise servers or applications. With no on-premise applications, there is little or no need for an on-premise Active Directory Domain Service. This type the organization can fully leverage the Azure Active Directory for its identity management, as the SaaS applications natively support it.

This allows the organization to greatly reduce cost and complexity, gaining the maximum benefit of the move to the cloud.

Design choice example:

• Azure Active Directory Basic.
• No On-Premise Active Directory Domain Services (AD DS).
• No Azure AD Connect.

This represents a truly cloud-optimized scenario, allowing the organization to fully leverage SaaS and PaaS applications at a greatly reduced cost.

Hybrid Identity Medium Scenario

For medium sized organizations, with larger on-premise footprints, on-premise based applications and servers, and more complex workstation management requirements, a hybrid design makes more sense. For these organizations, an on-premise Active Directory Domain Service likely exists and is supporting workstations and servers with group policies, traditional directory-aware applications, and centralized offices.

A hybrid design, including directory synchronization, allows the organization to retain the legacy infrastructure but leverage the Azure cloud for single sign-on between on-premise and cloud applications.

Design choice example:

• Azure Active Directory Premium P1.
• On-Premise Active Directory Domain Services (AD DS).

- Azure AD Connect hosted in Azure IaaS.
- Azure IaaS Backup of Azure AD Connect server for 1 hour recovery time.

This represents a standard hybrid-identity scenario.

Hybrid Identity Large Scenario

Large organizations will typically have a large on-premise infrastructure in multiple countries with an extensive catalog of traditional directory-aware line of business applications. A large organization, even with a cloud migration initiative, will typically be in a hybrid coexistence model for a long period. A hybrid design is essential to provide a seamless single sign-on experience for their users, as well include robust security requirements and fault tolerance to reduce the impact of outages.

A hybrid design, including directory synchronization, security features, and fault tolerance, will allow the organization to co-exist but leverage the Azure cloud features for single sign-on between on-premise and cloud applications, and provide an on-ramp to the cloud for traditional directory aware applications.

Design choice example:

- Azure Active Directory Premium P2.
- On-Premise Active Directory Domain Services (AD DS).
- Stretched Data Center with Azure IaaS Hosted AD DS domain controller.
- Azure AD Connect Primary server hosted in Azure IaaS.
- Azure AD Connect Staging server hosted in Azure IaaS.
- Azure IaaS Backup of Azure AD Connect server for 1 hour recovery time.

This represents an enterprise-grade hybrid-identity scenario.

It is important to consider many factors, including cloud-strategy, on-premise requirements, and application requirements when developing a hybrid identity design.

7 DESIGNING HYBRID NETWORKING

When designing a stretched datacenter, i.e. extending the existing on-premise data center to the Azure cloud, the networking is a critical design factor. Software defined networking (SDN) provides the abstraction and programmability to the traditional networking concepts, but requires a change in mindset from the rigid physical router, switch and circuits. The cloud networking brings a new level of flexibility and design capabilities, as well an ease of implementation unheard of in legacy networking.

Some of the networking elements and concepts to consider when designing Azure hybrid networking include Site-to-Site Virtual Private Networks, ExpressRoute, Virtual Networks, segmentation, and fault tolerance.

Software Defined Networking

Software Defined Networking is a virtualized networking model which abstracts the traditional physical elements such as cables, switches, routers, and gateways. This is analogous to the virtual machine, where the CPU, disk, memory, and network interfaces are virtualized versions of the physical systems.

SDN allows for dynamic management of all the aspect of networking, freeing designers from the constraints of physical systems. This also allows for centralized configuration, control, management, and global scaling.

An outcome of SDN is the ability to provision at cloud speed, creating and configuring elements like a switch or gateway in minutes rather than the weeks it would take to requisition, install, and configure physical devices.

Virtual Networks

An Azure Virtual Network (VNet) is the equivalent of a physical network switch, providing IP connectivity between Azure devices such as virtual machines. In addition, a VNet allow organizations to create subnets within the VNet, define DNS settings for members of the VNet, control traffic flows with Network Security Groups (NSGs) and route tables with user defined routing (UDR). VNets also provide services such as connectivity to the Internet, automatic Network Address Translation (NAT), and firewall protections against hackers.

Importantly, VNets can be connected to other VNets and on-premise network though Azure VPN Gateways or Virtual Appliances from organizations such as Cisco or Palo Alto Networks. Virtual appliances also allow for OSI layer 7 security models, such as Active Directory user based access control.

VPN Gateway

A Virtual Network Gateway routes traffic from within the VNet to an on-premise network. These routes can be either site-to-site for connecting to another network, on-premise or another VNet, or can be a point-to-site for connecting clients.

The VPN Gateway can be either a Virtual Private Network (VPN) Gateway which routes securely over the Internet using a Site-to-Site IPsec (Internet Protocol Security) tunnel or an ExpressRoute Gateway for a dedicated private connection.

S2S VPN

The Site-to-Site Virtual Private Network (S2S VPN) uses a connection over IPsec across the Public Internet. The tunnel goes from the Azure VNet Gateway to an on-premise network device, such as a Cisco Adaptive Security Appliance (ASA) or Microsoft Routing and Remote Access Server (RRAS). The tunnel is authenticated and secured by sophisticated encryption, creating a private tunnel between the Azure VNet and the on-premise network.

S2S connections are easy to setup, monitor and very cost effective. They have some bandwidth limitations, leading some organizations to consider the ExpressRoute option.

ExpressRoute

Alternatively, an organization can create an ExpressRoute dedicated private connection. This connection does not go over the Public Internet, but instead is provisioned by a connectivity provider between the organization and Microsoft. This is a direct physical connection, which allows for private communications, higher reliability, faster speeds, lower latencies, and higher security.

Setting up an ExpressRoute requires extensive planning, provisioning time, cost of connections and equipment, and typically a higher usage cost. Organizations with larger data transfer needs are typical consumers of this Azure service.

ExpressRoute connections typically have long lead times to provision due to the physical connections and coordination, measured in months in many cases.

Environment Segregation (Prod, Test, Development)

Many medium and large organizations have environments that require network segmentation, for regulatory reasons, for technical reasons, or for process reasons. This frequently includes the requirement to separate production from development and/or to maintain an isolated test environment. In an on-premise environment, this can frequently be a challenge for IT professionals, requiring extensive knowledge of VLAN technologies, purchase of equipment, or dedicating network ports to specific environments.

Azure SDN allows for easy provisioning, connection, securing, management, and monitoring of these different environments. The Azure networking components such as VNets, network security groups, user defined routing, and VNet-VNet connections allow designers to easily craft the exact connectivity and segmentation required, then implement it with minimal provisioning effort. This even includes extending the Azure environment segments to the appropriate on-premise environment segments, such as connecting the Azure production environment to the on-premise production environment and the Azure development environment to the on-premise development environment.

Fault Tolerance and Disaster Recovery

Many organizations have fault tolerance and disaster recovery networking design requirements. These can be regional requirements, such as the ability to fail over network connections from the Americas region to the Asia Pacific region. Or these can be local requirements, such as a specific VPN connection must fail over to a secondary on-premise device in the event of the primary device failure. Azure networking supports both design requirements.

To support regional fault tolerance requirements, Azure VNets can be created in different Azure regions such West US (located in California) and Southeast Asia (located in Singapore). Each of these VNets can have their own Virtual Gateway with a VPN connection to the on-premise network. In the event of a regional disaster (such as in California), traffic would still be routed from the other region (Singapore). This design provides the routing fault tolerance, as network routing protocols typically converge in seconds to recover from failed routes.

For local high availability fault tolerance requirements, there are several options both native and design element. For local high availability, the main options are:

- Active-Passive VPN Gateway – Each Azure VPN Gateway is implemented as a pair of virtual machines in an active-passive configuration. In the event of a disruption in the active virtual machine, the connection will fail over to the second virtual machine. This is the standard configuration.
- Multiple On-premises VPN devices – The Azure VPN Gateway can be configured with active connections to multiple on-premise VPN devices. In the event of a failure of one of the on-premise devices, the other connection would continue to route. Requires Border Gateway Protocol (BGP), which is a standard Internet routing protocol to support IP route failover.
- Active-Active Azure VPN Gateway – The on-premise can be configured with active connections to multiple Azure VPN Gateway connections. The Azure VPN Gateway virtual machines will both be active, each connecting to the same on-premise VPN device. In the event of a failure of one of the Azure gateway virtual machines, the other connection would continue to route.
- Dual-Redundancy – The two designs above (Multiple On-premises VPN devices and Active-Active Azure VPN Gateway) can be combined to create a full mesh of redundancy. Traffic flows between all 4 tunnels simultaneously. This option requires BGB to

be configured.

The options above are for organizations using VPN tunnels for connectivity. For large organizations that are using ExpressRoute private connections, there are primarily two options:

- Redundant Circuits – Each ExpressRoute is configured with two physical circuits to Microsoft at the connectivity provider facilities. These provide immediate local failover in the event of the loss of a single circuit.
- Redundant ExpressRoute – ExpressRoute can be provisioned in different regions, which will provide regional failover.

Azure networking provides a complete set of design options for fault tolerance and disaster recovery.

Hybrid Networking Small Scenario

For small organizations with a cloud-first strategy, hybrid networking would only be required to connect to Azure hosted services. Ideally, a small organization would be leveraging SaaS applications such as Office 365 for all its needs.

However, in some cases, there might be a need to connect to an Azure environment. Some examples might be a dedicated DevTest IaaS environment or a PaaS environment. In those cases, there would likely be a limited number of users.

Design choice example for a small organization:

- Azure VNet for Dedicated IaaS/PaaS environments.
- Azure VPN Gateway configured for Point-to-Site (P2S) connection.
- Clients connect using P2S VPN connections as needed.

This simplified model allows for flexible project based environments.

Hybrid Networking Medium Scenario

For medium sized organizations, with larger on-premise footprints, on-premise based applications and servers, and more complex workstation management requirements, a hybrid design makes more sense. For these organizations, an on-premise network likely exists and is supporting workstations and servers in centralized offices. In addition, there is likely a dedicated developer segmented network.

Full time connectivity and fault tolerance will be important design requirements, while reducing administrative overhead and cost factors.

Design choice example for a medium organization:

- Azure VNet for Production network.
- Azure VPN Gateway with a Site-to-Site (S2S) VPN connection to on-premise production network VPN device.
- Azure VNet for Developer network.
- Azure VPN Gateway with a S2S VPN connection to on-premise developer network VPN device.
- Active-Passive VPN Gateway Fault Tolerance.

This design example will support a typical medium sized organization complexity, throughput, segmentation, and fault tolerance requirements.

Hybrid Networking Large Scenario

Large organizations will typically have a large on-premise infrastructure in multiple countries with high bandwidth requirements for data transfers, migrations, and user access. A large organization, even with a cloud migration initiative, will typically be in a hybrid coexistence model for a long period. A hybrid design is essential to provide a seamless stretched datacenter experience for their users, as well include robust bandwidth, security requirements and fault tolerance to reduce the impact of outages.

A hybrid stretched data center design, including high bandwidth, segmentation, security features, and fault tolerance, will allow the organization to co-exist but leverage the Azure cloud features and provide an on-ramp to the cloud for data and applications.

Design choice example for a medium organization:

- Azure VNet for Production (Multiple/Regional)
- Azure VNet for Development (Multiple/Regional)
- Azure VNet for Test/QA (Multiple/Regional)
- Azure ExpressRoute (Regional)
- Azure VPN Gateways (Per VNet)
- Virtual Appliance (Per VNet)

A large organization will require a significantly more complex hybrid design, with extensive planning and lead time to establish.

8 DESIGNING DEVTEST ENVIRONMENTS

Providing development and test (DevTest) environments has been a headache for IT organizations, due to the rapidly changing requirements and proliferation. These DevTest environments are needed on short notice, may live for only a short period such as the life of a project, and have constantly shifting requirements. They are frequently driven by business-critical factors, giving IT little wiggle room to enforce compliance to standards without being seen as impeding the business.

Poorly managed development labs are often the source of hidden costs to the business, in the form of lost intellectual property when code is lost due to crashes, loss of valuable test data, and loss of productivity as the labs are rebuilt, code recreated, and test data regenerated.

Cloud based DevTest environments allow IT to meet those requirements by providing rapid deployment, flexible configuration, and even self-service capabilities to meet the business requirements cost effectively.

Azure DevTest Labs

Azure DevTest Labs provide a cloud based development and test environment with self-service, cost control features such as automatic shut down and quotas, custom images, and integrated networking.

In addition, the Azure DevTest Labs are integrated into development tools such as Team Services, plus have a Representational State Transfer (REST) API and a command line tool to provision from continuous integrations tools and orchestration tools.

Complex and Evolving Requirements

Many times, the development and test requirements are unclear and evolving. Business units or developers may not be sure on the direction a given project will take and are reluctant to limit themselves, so compensate by requesting far more than they need "just in case". And where requirements are known, those might change in unexpected ways once the project gets underway and development begins.

Frequently, extensive administrative control is required over the virtual machines and the resource environment, to allow for rapid changes if needed.

Ideally, the solution will allow a measure of self-service and control to be delegated to just the DevTest environment to allow flexibility to the developers and testers without compromising the control of the overall environment or other DevTest environments.

With Azure DevTest Labs, the organization can automate the provisioning of the environments based on specification, include templates for rapid deployment into the environment of key test harnesses, and allow for delegation to developers to make their own changes within their environment. With Azure DevTest Labs, existing environments can be duplicated to stamp out multiple identical test environments for scale out testing.

Network Segmentation

Segmentation of the development and testing environments can vary depending on the stage of the project. For example, during the initial development stages of the project, the developers will want an isolated network, i.e. a sandbox environment. During the later development stages of the project, the developers may want to connect to a more integrated environment like the development network. Finally, during the testing and quality assurance stages of the project, the testers may want to connect to a test network with quasi production services.

The network segmentation could take the form of separate DevTest environment requests or they might be requests to change the network connectivity of an existing environment.

These complex and changing network requirements make provisioning DevTest environments challenging. Azure DevTest Labs can be initially configured with their own isolated virtual network, providing for an isolated sandbox environment. That virtual network can then be connected to other virtual networks in Azure using VNet-VNet connections or even to on-premise development networks using the Azure VPN Gateway.

Self-Service, Quotas, and Policies

An important concept in DevTest environments is to allow flexibility to the users. They may have frequent changes, requests for new machines, reconfiguration of existing machines such as disk space or memory, and other changes. For example, a developer may be working on a piece of code in the middle of the night and find that the machine needs an additional 32 GB of RAM to run compile the code efficiently. The DevTest environment should be able to easily accommodate that request without having to stop the developer from working and not having to wake up an IT administrator to make the change.

Ideally, the developer should be able to make that change themselves via a self-service model. They should be able to go to the machine configuration and make that change quickly and effectively without having to create a high priority incident request.

Balancing this self-service and efficiency requirement is the need to control resource utilization and configuration. While self-service is beneficial to DevTest environments, limits need to be in place to ensure that resources are not consumed irresponsibly and that costs are contained. In addition, it is important to prevent incorrect configurations like connecting a DevTest environment to the production network. The Azure DevTest labs provide the security, role based access controls (RBAC), and policies to ensure that lab users have access and control over precisely what they need and no more.

Azure DevTest Labs include quotas that allow caps to be placed on the number of virtual machines that can be created, per lab, per group in a lab, or even per user in a lab. This allows lab users to create and configure their own resources, but keeps them within a lab budget to control sprawl. The DevTest labs can even be prepopulated with base images, common machine builds, tools that can be installed, and actions that can be taken against machines in the lab such clone or restarting. All of this provides an easy to use self-service interface

Backup and Recovery

In addition to controlling the lab environments, in some cases it is important to be able to backup and restore labs. Frequently, development environments are poorly managed and are not monitored or backed up due to limited resources or a view that the cost to manage is not justified for "non-production" environments. This can result in lost development time and intellectual property when a development environment crashes, as well as lost development productivity as the development environments are rebuilt. All of which translates to a cost to the business, albeit an often-hidden cost.

Fortunately, the level of effort and cost to backup the Azure DevTest Labs is very low. This can help prevent the loss of valuable development and testing time, allowing rapid restores of a development environment and return to productivity.

Well-managed development and test labs that provide both the self-service capabilities that developers want and control that IT needs are critical to organizations. Azure DevTest Labs provide that ease of deployment, self-service, integration, management, and fine grained control needed to support modern development and test labs.

9 BUILDING CLOUD INFRASTRUCTURE ON DEMAND

After organizations migrate basic commodity infrastructure to Software as a Service and Platform as a Service models, the remaining systems are typically servers and applications that will remain as virtual machines, and will be hosted in the cloud. In the cloud-based model, the typical steps to bring a server online and set it up can be streamlined with integrated tools built into Microsoft Azure. A traditional server deployment consists of installing the operating system manually from an ISO image, applying configurations, installing roles and features one-by-one, and working with the "networking team" to provide the desired connectivity. Leveraging the tools provided in Azure, this standard method of deployment can be greatly simplified through automation.

Organizations have a great opportunity to build their new processes incorporating these cloud scale automation techniques as they shift from a traditional on-premise datacenter to a cloud-based environment. This chapter covers several of the more common tasks and concepts developed into best practices that are used by organizations in the creation of the base infrastructure and network. These same concepts and tools are then used to deploy and manage application workloads, which is discussed in the next chapter.

Microsoft's "New" Model for Resource Deployment in Azure

For deploying resources in Azure, Microsoft has shifted from their original Azure Service Management (ASM) model—Azure Classic— to the Azure Resource Manager (ARM) model. The new ARM model provides a much better platform for integrating virtual machines, networking, storage, identity, and other Azure resources together.

Some of the core capabilities of the Azure Resource Manager model include:
- Resource Deployment and Management as a Group: ARM allows administrators to group together resources which have a similar lifecycle, to allow them to be managed as a cohesive unit (eg. a virtual machine with its storage, network interface and accompanying public IP address)
- Granular Role Based Access Control (RBAC) Integration: Security and management in the ARM model allows an administrator to use built-in roles, or create custom granular roles which can provide "just enough access" to the azure resources a developer or lower level administrator would need.
- Template Based Resource Definition and Deployment: ARM resources are defined and deployed with template files, based on an industry standard, JSON, file format. At its core, an ARM template consists of parameters, variables, resources and outputs.

```
{
    "$schema":  "http://schema.management.azure.com/schemas/2015-01-01/deploymentTemplate.json#",
    "contentVersion": "",
    "parameters": { },
    "variables": { },
    "resources": [ ],
    "outputs": { }
}
```

- Platform Agnostic Management Layer: Deploying and managing Azure resources in the portal, PowerShell, the Azure (cross-platform) CLI, or developer tools (Visual Studio) all use the same API's, which make transitioning between tool sets seamless. An ARM template can be written in Visual Studio, and deployed with PowerShell, the xplat CLI, or in the Azure portal. This promotes collaboration within and between teams/departments by allowing people to use the interface they are most comfortable with.

TEMPLATE

▦ Customized template
5 resources

✎ Edit   ⓘ Learn more

BASICS

* Subscription
Sandbox Environment ⌄

* Resource group ⓘ
◉ Create new   ◯ Use existing

* Location
West US ⌄

SETTINGS

* Admin Username ⓘ
marcus ✓

* Admin Password ⓘ
•••••••••••• ✓

* Dns Label Prefix ⓘ
heyvicki ✓

Windows OS Version ⓘ
2016-Datacenter ⌄

TERMS AND CONDITIONS

Azure Marketplace Terms | Azure Marketplace

By clicking "Purchase," I (a) agree to the applicable legal terms associated with the offering; (b) authorize Microsoft to charge or bill my current payment method for the fees associated the offering(s), including applicable taxes, with the same billing frequency as my Azure subscription, until I discontinue use of the offering(s); and (c) agree that, if the deployment involves 3rd party offerings, Microsoft may share my contact information and other details of such deployment with the publisher of that offering.

☑ I agree to the terms and conditions stated above

☐ Pin to dashboard

Purchase

Deploying a Windows Server VM in the Azure Portal from an ARM template written in Visual Studio

Building the Baseline Infrastructure to Extend the Datacenter to Azure

In building the base infrastructure in Azure, similar to how organizations deploy storage, networking, and virtualization host servers, Microsoft Azure has equivalent infrastructure pieces that need to be configured. Just like on-premise datacenters, one of the main components is the networking layer, creating the security and traffic boundaries for application to application communication, as well as isolation of communication both internally and externally. As discussed in a previous chapter, extending a standard on-premise environment—with a Microsoft Active Directory at its core—will typically require deploying one or more domain controllers in the new Azure environment for services like authentication/identity, security, DNS, and policy. Management servers ("admin workstations" or "jump boxes") can also be included as part of the base cloud environment infrastructure.

Configuring a Hybrid Network

While many implementations start with a few isolated test servers and applications deployed as a POC, the first step to building a true hybrid environment is configuring the networking layer. Most organizations want to extend their existing network to the cloud, which requires a hybrid network environment spanning between the on-premise and cloud environments.

The core components of the hybrid network include:
• Virtual network and subnets (deployed in azure)
• VPN/Tunneling: Site-to-Site (S2S) IPsec or ExpressRoute
• Firewall (optional)
• Network Security groups
• Routing

The following section expands on these components with real world scenarios and examples.

Creating and Configuring Virtual Network and Subnets in Microsoft Azure

The creation of virtual networks (VNets) and subnets is the starting point when deploying your software defined network (SDN). To begin, a VNet and one or more subnets within the VNet is created. For example:

A VNet in the Azure West US region is created, named vnet-WestUS, and a prefix of 10.4.0.0/16. Along with this VNet, 2 subnets within this VNet are also created, named Prod1 and Dev1, with prefixes 10.4.0.0/24 and 10.4.1.0/24 respectively.

This can be accomplished in the Azure portal, written as an ARM template and deployed in Visual Studio, or a combination of the two. To deploy their first VNet and subnets, an organization may choose use the Azure Portal as they are getting used to the concepts and methodology. Over time, they may expand this VNet with more subnets by writing a parameterized ARM template, allowing them to automate the process by passing in a subnet name and prefix as parameters at deployment time. This is a common approach which allows an organization to streamline their configuration and deployments as they gain more familiarity with the process.

```
1    {
2      "$schema": "https://schema.management.azure.com/schemas/2015-01-01/deploymentTemplate.json#",
3      "contentVersion": "1.0.0.0",
4  ⊞  "parameters": {…
47     },
48     "variables": {
49       "apiVersion": "2015-06-15"
50     },
51     "resources": [
52       {
53         "apiVersion": "[variables('apiVersion')]",
54         "type": "Microsoft.Network/virtualNetworks",
55         "name": "[parameters('vnetName')]",
56         "location": "[resourceGroup().location]",
57         "properties": {
58           "addressSpace": {
59             "addressPrefixes": [
60               "[parameters('vnetAddressPrefix')]"
61             ]
62           },
63           "subnets": [
64             {
65               "name": "[parameters('subnet1Name')]",
66               "properties": {
67                 "addressPrefix": "[parameters('subnet1Prefix')]"
68               }
69             },
70             {
71               "name": "[parameters('subnet2Name')]",
72               "properties": {
73                 "addressPrefix": "[parameters('subnet2Prefix')]"
74               }
75             }
76           ]
77         }
78       }
79     ]
80   }
```

A parameterized ARM template which deploys a VNet and two subnets, authored in Visual Studio Code

Creating and Configuring Connectivity between On-premise and Azure Networks

Connectivity between your existing on-premise network and the newly created Azure VNet is accomplished by setting up a Site-to-Site (S2S) VPN tunnel or ExpressRoute. Both scenarios can be configured in the Azure Portal or via an ARM template. At a high level, the process to create a standard S2S VPN tunnel consists of the following steps:

- Create a VNet in Azure – building block enabling the creation of gateway and resource subnets
- Create a gateway subnet in Azure – the IP addresses used by the VPN services will reside in this subnet
- Create a virtual network gateway in Azure – this process creates, among other things, the public IP address used to establish connectivity on the Azure side
- Create a local network gateway in Azure – this provides connectivity information about your on-premise environment, including the public IP used for its side of the VPN tunnel, as well as the private IPv4 address space(s) it services (your internal subnets)
- Configure your on-premise VPN device – create a new VPN connection in your on-prem VPN device, providing the public IP of your Azure gateway (from the previous step), and defining the tunnel security properties.
- Create a S2S VPN connection – the remaining step is setting up the VPN connection on the Azure side, specifying the VNet gateway, local network gateway, and the pre-shared secret (PSK).

Once these steps have been completed, Azure will begin the process of setting up the connection. The status can be verified in the portal, or with command line tools like Azure PowerShell.

Creating and Configuring Firewall Level Security

Firewalls can be deployed as virtual appliances within Azure, sitting in between your Azure VNet and the public internet or your on-premise network. To enhance their security posture, many organizations deploy one or more firewalls (for high availability) in a perimeter network (subnet), allowing only approved traffic in and out of the protected backend subnets. This allows for tight control, protecting the organization from untrusted networks, much like they do on-premise today with IDS and edge network appliances. The firewall appliance in Azure can also serve as the organizations VPN gateway/device to which the on-premise VPN device would connect and establish the S2S connectivity described previously.

Creating and Configuring Routes

Routing within Azure is approached in a similar manner to routing on premise, with a few additional considerations. As new networks/subnets are created on-premise or in Azure, an administrator may need to update the local/virtual network gateway address spaces to ensure resources on both sides can communicate as expected. Routes within Azure can also be created manually, known as user-defined routes (UDRs), and added to route tables to control the flow of traffic. UDRs can be used in a number of ways, but are a requirement in a scenario where all traffic must pass through a virtual firewall appliance, such as the topology described earlier where a backend app subnet sits behind a perimeter network, and is accessible only through the FW between them. This ensures all traffic must meet the requirements defined in the ACL, or in advanced scenarios (such as application firewalls), the user is permitted if they are a member of an approved security group. Managing URDs, route tables, and local/virtual network gateways can be done in the portal, via an ARM template, with the REST API, or via command line (e.g. Azure PowerShell).

Creating and Configuring Network Security Groups

In addition to UDRs and network (firewall) appliances, network security groups (NSGs) are an additional security boundary which allow the administrator to apply granular ACLs at different layers in the network topology. NSGs are simple stateful packet inspection devices which use the 5-tuple approach (source IP, source port, destination IP, destination port, and layer 4 protocol) to create allow/deny rules for traffic flows (https://docs.microsoft.com/en-us/azure/security/azure-security-network-security-best-practices#logically-segment-subnets). NSGs can be applied to an individual virtual machine network interface (NIC), the entire virtual machine, or at the subnet level. This allows broad policies to be applied to a set of servers in a subnet (at the subnet level - allow RDP over TCP/3389 from any internal network), and more tightly control ports which are VM/or application specific (at the VM level – allow TCP/1433 and 1434 from a subset of source IP's in your internal network). NSGs can be created and managed using any of the standard tools which interact with the ARM REST API, including the portal and Azure PowerShell.

3 Inbound security rules ⁺⁼

PRIORITY	NAME	SOURCE	DESTINATION	SERVICE	ACTION
100	Allow-External-IP	65.65.65.120/32	Any	Custom (Any/Any)	Allow
110	Allow-Intranet	10.4.0.0/16	Any	Custom (Any/Any)	Allow
500	Default-Deny	Any	Any	Custom (Any/Any)	Deny

Using the Azure Portal to view a "baseline" NSG

Deploying Core Services

Once the hybrid networking has been deployed, configured and tested, the next set of services can be built within the new infrastructure. The first workloads deployed are typically virtual machines. In an environment with identity managed by Microsoft Active Directory, the first VMs are usually

Domain Controllers. Building on the concepts from the previous chapter on identity, a few of the considerations and best practices with deploying DCs as VMs in Azure are:

- Decided if the DC in Azure needs to be a replica DC, or full blown global catalog. Questions which can help drive this decision are: Will the new Azure DCs be responsible for authentication? If so, is this a small subset of your existing user base, or most of the company? If a small subset of your user base will be authenticating against the Azure DC(s), a read-only domain controller with a small group of user's passwords cached locally will provide a balance between security and performance.
- For high availability, deploy at least two DC's in a virtual machine availability set. This will provide redundancy, in the event of planned, or unplanned maintenance within Azure. Using an availability set also enables an Azure load balancer to be placed in front of the VM's which can be used as a highly available DNS VIP, configured for your entire VNet or specific VM's.
- As with DC deployment on premise, it is best practice to store the AD database (SYSVOL) on separate drive from the operating system. In Azure, this concept is known as a "data disk".
- By default, virtual machines in Azure have dynamic IP addresses, akin to DHCP in an on-prem environment. When a VM is shut down and "deallocated", there is no guarantee it will have the same IP when it is powered back up. For this reason, configure your DC VMs with a reserved IP address.
- Azure VNets should be treated as "branch offices" and as such, should be set up as separate Active Directory sites. This means the pair of DC's deployed in an availability set in the West US region, in the "vnet-WestUS" VNet would be defined as "Azure West US" in Active Directory Sites and Services. This aligns with best practices, ensuring areas of high speed connectivity are configured as separate AD sites.

Workload Deployment and Testing

With the network and identity foundation in place, application deployments/testing can begin. Starting with a few simple workloads (before moving any real production apps/services) is a good approach for getting used to the deployment model and how connectivity works.

Virtual Machine Images

Many organizations spend time developing a "golden image" which includes packages, software, security updates, or other customizations. Azure provides the ability to upload your own custom image, which can be deployed via an ARM template or within the Azure Portal. For organizations looking to use resources which are pre-configured, the Azure Marketplace is a great ecosystem which provides readily available resources and images from Microsoft and other 3rd party vendors. A few examples of resources which can be easily deployed are: WordPress, MongoDB, Chef Server, Palo Alto Next Gen Firewall, and a Windows Server 2016 image with SQL Server 2016 Enterprise.

ARM templating and Automation

As discussed earlier, most—if not all—resources within Azure can be described in an ARM template and deployed. Tasks which are repeatable, and resources you'll deploy often should be automated as much as possible. This means spending time developing a set of foundational templates to deploy resources such as virtual machines, subnets, network security groups, websites, and SQL databases (PaaS). While the creation of virtual machines can be manually done, organizations can fully automate the end to end process—connecting it to the internal network, join the VM to the corporate domain, and layer on a standard configuration with the Desired State Configuration (DSC) virtual machine extension, or custom PowerShell post deployment script. This not only speeds up the process, but ensures deployments are consistent, with the right agents installed every time (SCOM, Chef, Puppet, antivirus). Virtual machine extensions allow deep integration with the guest operating system for post deployment tasks and automation activities, with many options available. Similar to the Azure Marketplace, VM extensions from both Microsoft and 3rd party vendors are available. Some of the more popular options are PowerShell DSC, Chef, custom PowerShell script extension, and anti-virus agents such as Symantec's Endpoint Protection. Desired State Configuration can be managed with a traditional Windows Server, with nodes configured for either Push or Pull. Alternatively, Azure also provides a service, Azure Automation DSC, which takes the complexity out of managing DSC, and provides rich reporting, onboarding and management functionality over the entire environment.

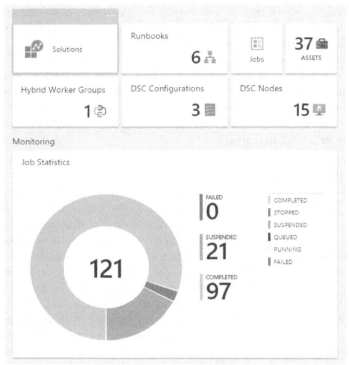

Azure Automation DSC overview blade from the portal

Tying it All Together

A few examples on how the concepts in this chapter work together.

Deploying a Windows Server VM

A typical example of a workload which is deployed often is a Windows server VM. In this scenario, an ARM template can be created, and parameterized providing a balance between automation and dynamic deployment. At deployment time, a user would have the following options available to them:

- VM name: Dynamic user input field
- OS Version: Configured with a default option (Windows Server 2016), and allows the user to select from an approved list of images (eg. Windows Server 2012R2).
- Subnet: Configured with a default option ("Server-Subnet"), and allows the user to select from a fixed list of subnets within the virtual network.

- Network Security Group — Configured with a default "baseline" option ("Corp-Server-NSG"), and allows the user to select from a fixed list of NSGs which meet their requirements (Web Server NSG, SQL Server NSG).

As discussed, the VM can be deployed from the organization's custom image, or from a standard Microsoft image in the gallery.

The methodology here is to hard code areas of your template which are not subject to change, and use parameters for items which should be user driven at deployment time.

Other components like domain join, role/feature installation, agents which are typically deployed should be accomplished with Desired State Configuration, VM extensions, or a custom Azure Automation Runbook.

Deploying a SQL VM

Beyond the creation of a simple Windows VM for business application purposes, most organizations have a need to backend their applications with a database. These deployments are typically very time consuming, long running, and subject to missed steps due to the number of items which make up a "baseline" deliverable (backups configured, patching, drive layout, permissions, etc.). This type of deployment can also be fully automated using the techniques described in this chapter.

The Azure Marketplace provides a full suite of Microsoft SQL Server virtual machines, with a combination of various OS versions (WS 2012R2, WS2016) and versions of SQL (enterprise/standard in 2012, 2014, 2016).

By leveraging these images, any administrator can walk through the process of deploying a fully configured SQL server, selecting their required options/preferences

- Standard VM options: VM size (# of CPU cores, total RAM, SSD vs. HDD), subnet, network security group, VM extensions
- SQL specific options:
    - Authentication: SQL vs. Windows
    - Performance/Storage requirements: # of IOPS required, throughput in MBs, storage footprint (in TB's), and workload profile (general, OLTP, or data warehousing)
    - Patching: enable/disable automated scheduled patching, specifying day of the week preference, maintenance windows start time and duration
    - Backup: enable/disable automated backup, retention period, encryption of backups, and backup schedule preference

Once an organization has standardized on a set of "baseline" requirements, the configuration preferences can be exported as an ARM template, and resused for future deployments. The same parameterization techniques can be used, allowing for user-input in the areas which should be dynamic (eg. host name).

Using the SQL virtual machine image also allows the performance (# IOPS) to be scaled up at any time (even after deployment) from within the portal. Accomplishing the same task on-premise can be very challenging and time consuming.

Azure Network

To get a sense of the scale at which ARM templates can automate deployments, the screenshot below is a 1000+ line template, which consistently deploys an entire Azure network, end to end, with no end user intervention. After populating the corresponding parameter file with the desired names, subnet prefixes, etc., the deployment starts, and roughly 30 minutes later the end result is a fully configured Azure VNet, three subnets, granular network security groups, user defined routes, and a Palo Alto Networks Next-Gen Firewall at the center of it all.

```
template.json ●
{
    "$schema": "https://schema.management.azure.com/schemas/2015-01-01/deploymentTemplate.json#",
    "contentVersion": "1.0.0.13",
    "parameters": {···
    },
    "variables": {···
    },
    "resources": [
        {"type": "Microsoft.Resources/deployments",
            "name": "PAN-VM",
            "apiVersion": "2015-01-01",
            "properties": {···
            },
            "dependsOn": [
                "Microsoft.Resources/deployments/SettingUpStorageAccount",
                "Microsoft.Resources/deployments/SettingUpPublicIPs",
                "[concat('Microsoft.Network/networkSecurityGroups/',parameters('NSG-Untrust-Name'))]
                "Microsoft.Resources/deployments/SettingUpVirtualNetwork",
                "Microsoft.Resources/deployments/SetupNetworkInterfaces"
            ]
        },
        {"type": "Microsoft.Network/virtualNetworkGateways",···
        },
        {"type": "Microsoft.Resources/deployments",···
        },
        {"type": "Microsoft.Resources/deployments",···
        },
        {"type": "Microsoft.Network/networkSecurityGroups",···
        },
        {"type": "Microsoft.Network/networkSecurityGroups",···
        },
        {"type": "Microsoft.Resources/deployments",···
        },
        {"type": "Microsoft.Resources/deployments",···
        },
        {"type": "Microsoft.Network/routeTables",···
        },
        {"type": "Microsoft.Network/routeTables",···
        },
        {"type": "Microsoft.Network/publicIPAddresses",···
        }
    ]
```

ARM template which fully automates an end to end Azure network deployment

These examples should highlight the benefits of fully embracing the automation and configuration options available within Azure. These, and other ARM template examples are in the book's GitHub code repo.

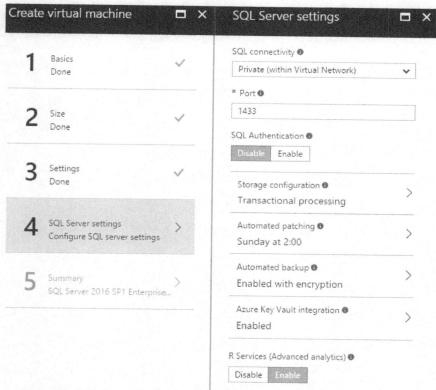

Deploying a SQL VM using an image from the Azure Marketplace

10 MIGRATING APPLICATIONS TO THE CLOUD

The last chapter covered building the core infrastructure needed to support a typical enterprise environment's applications, including a hybrid network, domain controllers for identity, and introduced cloud automation techniques. With the core components in place, application workloads are the next target in the migration to Azure.

As previously highlighted, the focus isn't to immediately replicate existing infrastructure from on-premise to the cloud. The same concept applies to the migration of applications. The organization should look at this exercise as a perfect opportunity to take a step back, evaluate the applications as they exist today, and determine the best method and options for moving these services to the cloud.

Decisions Impacting the Migration Approach

For each application (and its underlying servers), there are key decisions which help determine the best migration approach. These decisions guide the organization's choices, allowing them develop a plan of action.

Leveraging Platform as a Service (PaaS) as an Application Migration Strategy

While many organizations think of a migration of an application involving the movement of the entire server to the cloud as the primary method (OS, application, and its data), the Platform as a Service model (PaaS) can provide a tremendous amount of value, even if replacing a single tier within the app. Replacing one or more of an app's tiers from the traditional virtual machine, Infrastructure as a Service (IaaS) model with PaaS can help reduce the footprint and management overhead for the application and operation admins.

When evaluating if the application is a good candidate to fit the PaaS model, the types of questions the key decision makers need to ask and evaluate are:

- Does the application use standard web services (eg. .NET, Apache, Node.js, PHP) – If so, there's a good possibility of simply porting the application over to Azure App Services and retiring the web server functionality within the VM(s).
- Does the application logic rely on a standard enterprise data layer (eg. MS SQL server, MySQL, MongoDB) – If so, moving this tier to PaaS would consist of migrating the schema and data from the on-prem server to Microsoft's SQL PaaS service, Azure SQL or their NoSQL PaaS service, DocumentDB.
- Does the organization have access to the source code to export/import to any similarly configured web or database platform?

Utilizing PaaS does not have to be an all or nothing approach. A multi-tier application with a web front end, application logic and database backend can be reconfigured into intermixed IaaS VMs and PaaS services, where the web tier is ported to PaaS, and the app/database layer deployed to an Azure VM availability set. Every component the organization can strip away from the virtual machine layer, which requires the most oversight and manual administration (monthly patching, agent installations, storage upkeep, etc.) allows the organization to reduce its overhead, and focus their time and effort on other value add areas.

Moving to a Platform as a Service (PaaS) Model

Moving a traditional multi-tier application completely to a PaaS model consists of finding the equivalent services which provide the same (or better) set of features. For example, an app which has a web front end, application logic and database hosted on one or more VMs can be a great opportunity to take advantage of Azure PaaS services. Translating the tiers to PaaS may look like:

- Tier → PaaS Service → Azure Offering
- Web → PaaS Web Apps → Azure App Service
- App → PaaS [serverless] Compute → Azure Functions or Azure Logic Apps
- Data → PaaS DB → Azure SQL

The process of breaking apart an application (decoupling) and moving its components to PaaS can seem like a daunting effort. Fortunately, there are many tools, such as migration wizards, which can aide in the process, even providing helpful warning or error messages when a component isn't compatible, or needs to be reconfigured.

Web App Migration

To migrate a simple website or app from a Windows server running IIS, Microsoft provides a migration wizard, "Web Apps Migration Assistant", which analyzes your site, highlights areas which have compatibility issues or cannot be migrated, and guides you through the process of moving your content up to Azure. This wizard can move both the website, and its underlying databases, provided both are compatible and ready to move.

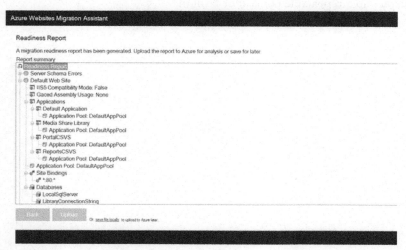

The readiness report generated after the web app migration wizard has analyzed a server's websites

Application Logic Migration

The process of moving the application logic layer can arguably be the most difficult. This is the area which does most of the heavy lifting, performing complex operations, connecting users from the frontend, to the data in the backend. In a lot of cases, the process to move this layer up to PaaS often does not have a direct "migration wizard" approach available. Often, the application layer will need to be broken out into a group of discrete "functions" each performing a specific task. Once the organization has landed on a set of functions which need to be performed between the presentation and data layers, they can be ported over to PaaS. Azure's serverless compute offering known as Azure Functions provides the ability to run code (functions) written in many languages such as Python, JavaScript, C#, PHP, PowerShell, and F#. Azure also provides a platform to host API apps, which can serve as the logic layer in your stack. To stitch these discrete functions and API's together into a cohesive unit, tools like Azure API Management and Azure Logic Apps help bring these components together, providing a robust modular middle tier. Azure Logic Apps enable an organization to bring their own custom code (API's or functions), consume Microsoft services, or connect 3rd party services together. These apps can be developed in the Azure Portal or Visual Studio, and deployed with ARM templates, like a standard Azure resource. This allows an organization to easily build complex integration applications which can typically take weeks or months, templatize the entire thing, and deploy in a repeatable consistent fashion.

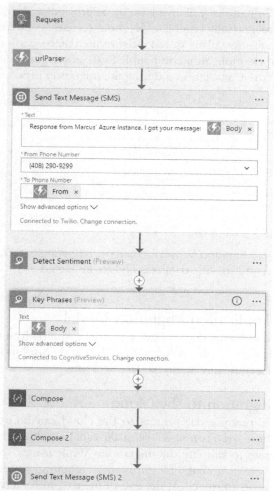

Logic App Designer View

Database Migration

Migrating a database up to Azure SQL can also be broken out into a series set of steps, and handled in a separate migration phase. This allows the database schema to be verified, reconfigured (if required) and migrated up to Azure SQL, before any data is transferred. The process of migrating the data can also be handled in a series of steps, with an initial sync taking place first, and one (or more) delta syncs taking place closer to the actual cutover. The most common method of moving a SQL database up to Azure SQL is using the open source "SQL Database Migration Wizard". While the tool does a lot of the heavy lifting for the user, known compatibility issues and limitations will need to be addressed and fixed before the migration can successfully complete. In some scenarios, an error can be ignored, if the organization plans to reconfigure the database after it is moved up to Azure. For example, in incompatible SQL stored procedure can be rewritten after migrating, and ignored during the migration process.

Table [dbo].[Employees] -- Removed 'NOT FOR REPLICATION' because it is not supported in this version of SQL Server.
Table [dbo].[Employees] -- Removed 'not for replication' because it is not supported in this version of SQL Server.
Table [dbo].[Employees] -- Removed 'not for replication' because it is not supported in this version of SQL Server.
Table [dbo].[Employees] -- Removed 'not for replication' because it is not supported in this version of SQL Server.
Changing index [dbo].[Companies].aaaaaCompanies_PK to a clustered index. You may want to pick a different index to cluster on.

Table [dbo].[Companies] -- Removed 'NOT FOR REPLICATION' because it is not supported in this version of SQL Server.
Table [dbo].[Companies] -- Removed 'not for replication' because it is not supported in this version of SQL Server.
Table [dbo].[Companies] -- Removed 'not for replication' because it is not supported in this version of SQL Server.
Table [dbo].[Companies] -- Removed 'not for replication' because it is not supported in this version of SQL Server.
StoredProcedure [dbo].[ContactTotalsReport] -- Deprecated feature 'Table hint without WITH'. Automatically added WITH for you.
StoredProcedure [dbo].[ContactTotalsReport] -- Deprecated feature 'Table hint without WITH'. Automatically added WITH for you.
StoredProcedure [dbo].[ContactTotalsReport] -- Deprecated feature 'Table hint without WITH'. Automatically added WITH for you.
StoredProcedure [dbo].[ContactTotalsReport] -- Deprecated feature 'Table hint without WITH'. Automatically added WITH for you.
StoredProcedure [dbo].[ContactTotalsReport] -- Deprecated feature 'Table hint without WITH'. Automatically added WITH for you.
StoredProcedure [dbo].[ContactTotalsReport] -- Deprecated feature 'Table hint without WITH'. Automatically added WITH for you.

Results from the SQL Migration Wizard's analysis, reporting errors, corrective action, and specific database objects impacted

Lift and Shift as an Application Migration Model

When the key decision questions do not indicate a successful path to the PaaS model, the organization is very likely left with a "Lift and Shift" model of moving an existing application server and its data to Azure.

Automation in the Migration to the Cloud

The migration from on-premise datacenters to the cloud can be done manually, one VM at a time, or economies of scale can be achieved by creating automated processes to simplify the migration. While it may seem like every application environment is different, requiring unique considerations and a hands-on approach, at the end of the day, most servers boil down to a set of core similarities—same backup, management and monitoring agents installed, similar operating systems, connected to the corporate network— which enable the organization to bake these properties into an automated framework, allowing the process of moving the VM's to be streamlined. This also dramatically reduces the time and effort required to batch and move workloads up to Azure.

Implementing Best Practices

As discussed previously, the migration effort is a great opportunity to not only move to the cloud, but a chance to implement best practices which were never considered, costly, time consuming, or difficult to do in an on-premise environment. This allows the organization to add a ton of value to their VM workloads immediately after the migration, rather than a "same stuff different datacenter" scenario. A few areas where a simple VM migration to Azure can be enhanced are:

Marketplace Images

Using the Azure Marketplace to deploy workloads which will remain as virtual machines (SQL servers) is a great opportunity to benefit from the automation capabilities built into the offering. Retiring legacy SQL 2005/2008 servers, and deploying new 2014/2016 replacements from a gallery image can be as simple as backing up the database(s), and restoring them in the new VM.

Automation

Leveraging services like Azure Automation DSC to apply and report on a baseline configuration across the entire environment is a great first step into "Configuration as Code". Over time, DSC can be leveraged in more robust application specific areas, but starting with something as simple as ensuring all Windows servers have a SCOM agent installed and configured is an easy win.

Reports

TYPE	STATUS	REPORT TIME
Consistency	✔ Compliant	4/3/2017, 10:36 AM
Consistency	✔ Compliant	4/3/2017, 10:36 AM
Consistency	✔ Compliant	4/3/2017, 10:21 AM
Consistency	✔ Compliant	4/3/2017, 10:06 AM
Consistency	✔ Compliant	4/3/2017, 10:06 AM
Consistency	✔ Compliant	4/3/2017, 9:51 AM
Consistency	✔ Compliant	4/3/2017, 9:36 AM
Consistency	✔ Compliant	4/3/2017, 9:36 AM
Consistency	✔ Compliant	4/3/2017, 9:21 AM
Consistency	✘ Failed	4/3/2017, 9:07 AM
Consistency	✔ Compliant	4/3/2017, 8:48 AM
Consistency	✔ Compliant	4/3/2017, 8:33 AM
Consistency	✔ Compliant	4/3/2017, 8:33 AM
Consistency	✔ Compliant	4/3/2017, 8:18 AM

Report status
✔ Compliant

Report time
4/3/2017, 10:36 AM

Start time
4/3/2017, 10:36 AM

Total runtime
2 seconds

Type
Consistency

Resources

xRemoteFile	✔ Compliant
Package	✔ Compliant
Service	✔ Compliant

Node state at report time
Node name
SCORCH01

IP address
10.4.0.45

Configuration mode
Apply and monitor

Health report from a server connected to Azure Automation DSC, with a configuration applied which installs the OMS agent

Auto-Scaling

Using a virtual machine scale set, Azure provides the ability to auto scale

63

a group of VM's based on KPI's selected by the admin. For a simple web tier, which all run the same configuration, if connections suddenly spike, and sustain over a period of time, additional servers can be automatically spun up, configured, and added to a load balancer with zero intervention by the app owner or operations team. This is a great feature, not easily reproduced in an on-prem scenario, which can be introduced when moving web service VMs up to Azure.

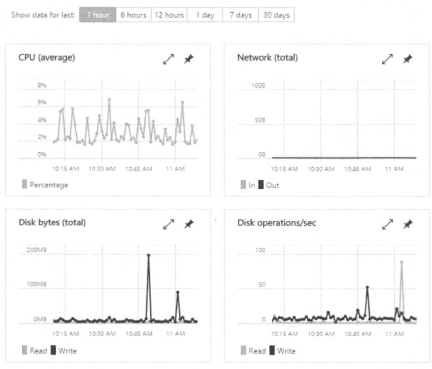

Integrated VM performance statistics from within the Azure Portal

Backups

Azure provides a first-class experience for virtual machine backups, which can be fully automated. A baseline backup policy can be created, and applied to all VM's in the subscription to ensure they meet the minimum organization requirements (eg. daily incremental, and weekly full backups). Along with an easy onboarding experience, granular on-demand restoration of files/folders or entire VM's is also provided within the same recovery services offering. Backups (and restorations) can be a major pain point for organizations, which can be simplified as part of the move to the Azure cloud.

Azure Backup service showing a high level overview of the VMs currently under protection

Web Services

As part of the move to the cloud, web servers are a great candidate for implementing modern best practices. Storing a web server's configuration in source control allows for easy redeployment of a production server, or spinning up a dev/test server based on the same code base to POC a new change. Reconfiguring a website to take advantage of Azure cloud delivery network (CDN) functionality to enable performance and user experience optimization should also be considered (in both IaaS and PaaS scenarios). Other services which can be layered on top of a simple web server in Azure which would traditionally cost thousands of dollars in an on-premise environment are Azure Traffic Manager and virtual machine load balancers. When used together, these services can enable simple round robin load balancing, or geo-routed application delivery to end users, directing a user's session traffic to a web server in the region closest to them.

11 MANAGING THE CLOUD INFRASTRUCTURE AND ENVIRONMENT

After the cloud infrastructure has been built, organizations still need to manage the cloud virtual machines, operating systems, and network connections that includes patching, administering and managing the systems. Depending on the deployment model selected, that management may be significant and require management applications as the cloud environment scales up. It is critical for the organization to factor that into the cloud model selection, migration of applications, and to design the appropriate management systems needed.

Why manage the cloud?

A common misconception is that once an organization moves to the cloud, there is no longer any need to manage the systems or applications. Depending on the model chosen, there could be a considerable amount of patching, software deployment, configuration management, and other management needed in a cloud environment.

Managing IaaS vs PaaS vs SaaS

The different cloud models of Infrastructure-as-a-Service (IaaS), Platform-as-a-Service (PaaS), and Software-as-a-Service (SaaS) are all used by organizations as they transition to the cloud. The management of the different cloud models is very different.

With IaaS, the organization is essentially using computing infrastructure in the cloud. This includes virtual servers, CPU, memory, storage, networking, etc. In this model, the cloud provider, such a Microsoft Azure, manages the IaaS hosting infrastructure (physical hardware, networking, etc.). The organization manages the IaaS operating system, middleware, and applications. This IaaS model gives the organization more management control, but requires more management overhead.

With PaaS, the organization is essentially using services in the cloud. This includes database services, web services, data analytics services, etc. In this model, the cloud provider, such a Microsoft Azure, manages the physical hosting infrastructure, operating system, and middleware. The organization manages the applications. This PaaS model gives the organization less management control, but also far less management overhead.

Finally, with SaaS, the organization is using a cloud based application. In this model, the cloud provider, such a Microsoft Office 365, manages everything including the physical hosting infrastructure, operating system, middleware, and the application. The organization just uses the applications. This SaaS model gives the organization no management control, but also no management overhead.

Given the management characteristics of each cloud model, the only model requiring significant management effort to patch, manage configuration, etc., is the IaaS model. However, IaaS is the model that many IT organizations might drive to initially, to avoid having to modernize applications by refactoring them into PaaS or SaaS offerings. Just forklifting applications into IaaS and not modernizing might get an organization to the cloud, but not result in the management savings that the cloud can offer.

However, for many organizations, IaaS will be a fact of life. Thus, decisions need to be made on how to manage the cloud infrastructure and environment. The next sections will look at the various options available.

Patching

For patching IaaS, there are a variety of options, which are very similar to the options of patching on-premise workloads. These include manual or operating system controlled patching, centralized update services like Windows Update Server (WSUS), cloud based services like Operations Management Suite (OMS), or full blown systems management tools like Microsoft System Center Configuration Manager (SCCM). With IaaS, the workloads are essentially just virtual machines hosted in a cloud data center, which is not much different from a management perspective than virtual machines hosted in an on-premise data center.

- Manual or Operating System Controlled Updates – Modern operating systems such as Microsoft Windows Server 2016 or Linux have built-in patching mechanisms. For Microsoft, there is the Automatic Updates feature and for Linux, there is the GNOME Update Manager as well as other tools. These allow the operating system to automatically select and install patches. This is simple and convenient to setup, but provides little centralized control or reporting as all servers operate independently of each other. Administrators cannot easily select which updates get applied without interacting with the server directly.

- Windows Server Update Services (WSUS) – For a more centralized and controlled approach, an update service like WSUS allows for centralized approval and reporting of updates and status. Administrators can select which updates are approved and the servers install them automatically. However, administrators cannot easily change the installation time, as it is typically a set schedule. This is a useful service when centralized control of patches is needed, but not of implementation times.

- Operations Management Suite (OMS) – The Microsoft Azure OMS provides centralized reporting and deployment of patches to both Windows and Linux servers. This allows administrators to see the patching state of all the servers in a single pane of glass. And it allows implementation of patches to be scheduled for groups of servers, allowing for a measure of control over implementation times. The disadvantage of OMS patching is that it does not allow for the selection of which patches to install, though this could be controlled in combination with WSUS.

- System Center Configuration Manager (SCCM) – For the highest level of control for both patch selection and implementation timing, SCCM provides the best features for both Windows and Linux Servers. SCCM allows administrators to select different patches for different groups of servers, as well as deploy those patches on whatever schedule works best for the organization. SCCM even allows groups of computers to be patched in sequence, ensuring that each server completes its patching before the next server is patched. For the most administrative flexibility and control over the patching of servers, SCCM is the tool to deploy.

Each of the example options given above have trade-offs between the level of control over what patches to apply and when to apply them, and how much administrative overhead there is in managing the process.

Software Deployment

When managing a handful of IaaS virtual machines, software deployment is straightforward and can be handled manually. When managing larger numbers of IaaS virtual machines, software deployment needs to be managed using tools to accommodate packaging, automatic deployment, monitoring deployments, reporting on deployment status. These software deployment tools can be custom developed scripts in simple cases or full blown management suites like Microsoft System Center.

- Manual Deployment – Manual deployment is an option for small numbers of servers. Copying software packages from a central repository and running them on the target IaaS virtual machine works, but the level of effort quickly gets out of hand for more than a couple servers. This will only work for the smallest of organizations, due to the lack of automation and centralized reporting.

- PowerShell – PowerShell can also be used to automate the deployment of software to larger numbers of IaaS virtual servers. Either PowerShell remote, PowerShell Desired State Configuration (DSC), or Azure Automation, can be used to create scripts to deploy software to servers. This enables automation, remote deployment, and centralized control to reduce the level of effort and improve the manageability of larger numbers of servers. However, this also requires a significant investment in script development, both in the initial development and maintenance of the scripts ongoing. While logging can be built into the scripts, reporting can be a challenge as well as long term monitoring of deployment states.

- System Center Configuration Manager (SCCM) – For the highest level of control for software deployment, a systems management tool such as SCCM provides the best features for both Windows and Linux Servers. SCCM allows administrators to control the deployment of software for different groups of servers, as well as deploy the software on whatever schedule works best for the organization. SCCM will also report immediate status of a given software deployment, allowing administrators to track the percentage complete, in progress, or failed. For the most administrative flexibility and control over software deployment servers, SCCM is the tool to deploy.

While the manual approach works for small numbers of servers, as organizations scale up either scripted or systems management tools will be needed to deploy software to IaaS workloads easily and reliably.

Configuration Management

When IaaS machines are deployed properly, they will be secured and tuned with the proper configuration settings. These setting can be registry settings, updates, software installed, services disabled, and other server and application settings. However, over time, machines experience configuration drift, meaning the configuration settings change due to maintenance, updates, testing, or other routine activities. These changes could also be the result of malicious actors. This configuration drift results in IaaS machines that are not secure or performing as expected.

Configuration management monitors, alerts on, and remediates this configuration drift. Configuration management can include manual methods, built in Azure tools, script methods, and systems management tools.

- Manual – For small number of IaaS machines, it is possible to check the configuration manually. Organizations doing this typically have a printed checklist and will review servers manually on a set schedule. As the number of servers scales up, this can be very time consuming and prone to error.

- Azure Security Center – The Azure Security Center monitors IaaS virtual machines with an eye towards security configurations, including policy driven monitoring, behavioral analysis, and remediation for key configuration gaps. Policies include system updates, operating system vulnerabilities, encryption settings, network security, and other key configurations. It will also alert for any configuration issues. The policies are not very customizable and can only be turned on or off, making it less suitable for large organizations with diverse workloads.

- PowerShell – PowerShell scripting can be used to manage the configuration of IaaS virtual servers. Either PowerShell remote, PowerShell Desired State Configuration (DSC), or Azure Automation, can be used to create scripts to manage configuration of servers. This enables automation, remote deployment, and centralized control to reduce the level of effort and improve the manageability of larger numbers of servers. PowerShell DSC was designed for that specific purpose. However, this scripting approach requires a significant investment in script development, both in the initial development and maintenance of the scripts ongoing.

- Operations Management Suite (OMS) – The Microsoft Azure OMS provides centralized configuration management through the Change Tracking solution to both Windows and Linux servers. This includes software, Windows services, Linux daemons, Windows registry settings, both Windows and Linux files. This is a very scalable service for monitoring configuration changes and has an excellent dashboard view, but remediation is somewhat clunky as it uses alerts and Azure Automation Runbooks to implement. It also has a limited one-size-fits-all configuration, where it manages the same configuration setting across all virtual machines.

- System Center Configuration Manager (SCCM) – For the highest level of control for configuration management, a systems management tool such as SCCM provides the best features for both Windows and Linux Servers. With SCCM, administrators can manage any configuration setting, including registry, operating system, files, folders, services, installed software, or any other setting. And the configuration can be monitored on a flexible schedule, ranging from minutes to days. The settings can be managed very granularly, allowing groups of servers to be monitored for different settings. And setting can be remediated automatically, allowing for self-healing configuration management. SCCM provides administrative flexibility and control over the configuration management of servers of any of the options.

Configuration management is an often-overlooked component of managing IaaS workloads, but is key to the long-term health, performance, and security of systems. Choosing the appropriate configuration management method is a critical task.

Management Small Scenario

For small organizations with a cloud-first strategy, they will ideally be leveraging SaaS applications such as Office 365 for all its needs. As such, there should be only a handful of IaaS servers needing management.

For those few IaaS servers, the small organization will want to leverage manual or built-in solutions.

Design choice example for a small organization:

- Operating System controlled updates directly to the vendor. In the case of Windows, this would be Automatic Updates.
- Software deployed manually.
- Azure Security Center for configuration management.

This simplified model allows for low cost and low effort management of the small number of servers.

Management Medium Scenario

For medium sized organizations, more automated methods will be required to manage the larger numbers of IaaS servers. This needs to include centralized management of updates, software, and configuration, while reducing administrative overhead and cost factors.

Design choice example for a medium organization:

- For updates, OMS strikes a good balance between centralization, reporting, and ease of deployment.
- Software deployment can be done using Manual Deployment for smaller numbers of servers or PowerShell for larger numbers of servers.
- For configuration management, OMS for monitoring

configuration settings and PowerShell DSC for remediating configuration settings.

This design example will support a typical medium sized organization, with a reasonable number of IaaS workload with a reasonably moderate level of effort.

Management Large Scenario

Large organizations will typically have a large on-premise infrastructure in multiple countries with IaaS servers both on premise and in the cloud. A large organization, even with a cloud migration initiative, will typically be in a hybrid coexistence model for a long period. A design supporting the hybrid model is essential to provide a seamless stretched datacenter experience for administration.

Enterprise organizations will also have many IaaS servers, both in the cloud and on-premise. These servers could very well include Windows and Linux versions. In addition, the servers will have different patching, software, and configuration requirements, requiring the solution to be flexible as well.

A large organization will require an enterprise grade system management solution, which will typically handle all aspects of management.

Design choice example for a large organization:

- SCCM is the best choice for a large organization to flexibly manage updates, software deployments, and configurations across Azure cloud and on-premise Windows and Linux IaaS workloads.

Having a single integrated system management solution like SCCM will provide the best options for a large organization.

12 MONITORING THE CLOUD INFRASTRUCTURE ENVIRONMENT

As applications and systems shift from historical datacenters to cloud-based services and resources, the shift to cloud-based monitoring systems also begins to make sense. Many organizations simply migrate their monitoring servers to the cloud as virtual machines, however if you step back and realize that those monitoring systems weren't built for cloud-based datacenters, that unless the application has been completely rewritten to be effective in a cloud-based environment, it might be time to look into a cloud-based monitoring system built ground up to manage modern systems and services.

OMS, A Single Pane of Glass Across All Environments

Microsoft Operations Management Suite (OMS) is a cloud based solution designed to manage the cloud and more. OMS characteristics include:

- Minimal Complexity to Deploy
- Minimal Cost to Deploy
- Scales to Cloud Levels
- Developed and Updated at Cloud Speed
- Deeply Integrated with Azure
- Completely Browser Based Access

Because it is hosted in the cloud, it can be deployed at cloud speed and be up and running in minutes. There is even a free tier, so start-up cost can be zero. This is in stark contrast to on-premise monitoring solutions, which typically take weeks and months to get up and running.

The range of management functions that the OMS license covers consists of Log Analytics, Automation, Backup, and Site Recovery. However, Log Analytics is the mainstay of the OMS functionality. In effect, Log Analytics collects data from a wide range of sources and stores the data in a cloud scale repository. The data is then available for alerting, analysis, reporting, and exporting. Data sources include Windows/Linux operating systems, Azure services, and even a Data Collector API, which enables data from any source to be uploaded.

The data is then presented in a set of sophisticated views and dashboards, which are organized into solutions covering areas or technologies. There is also a generalized query interface, which allows the data repository to be rapidly searched and visualized. Alerts can be generated when key conditions are met, as defined by queries, and automation actions can be triggered as well.

OMS provides a single pane of glass from which to manage all the organizations environments, including:

- Azure Cloud
- On-Premise
- Third-Party Hosted

OMS is a natural fit for Azure, as in many cases it is a simple 1-click option to enable integration with an OMS workspace. The image below shows virtual machines connection status, but they can be added by simply clicking on the server to begin the agent install.

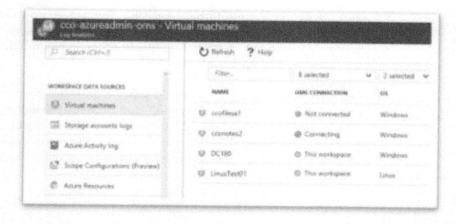

OMS can monitor any virtual machines, storage accounts, Azure activity logs, and any Azure resource.

OMS also integrates with on-premise System Center Operations Manager (SCOM) installations, leveraging the installed base of SCOM agents. When using this hybrid mode, the SCOM agents forward their information to the OMS workspace in addition to the SCOM management group. The integration is particularly easy, since no individual server configuration is needed, it does not impact the existing SCOM agents, and the communication is very efficient. Where there is no SCOM infrastructure, OMS agents can be installed on the on-premise servers.

For other environments, such as Amazon Web Services or other 3rd Party Hosted environments, Windows and Linux IaaS servers can have OMS agents installed and they will forward their information to the OMS workspace.

Security Threat Monitoring

OMS provides extensive capabilities to manage the myriad of security threats facing modern organizations and clouds. Security oriented solutions that OMS provides include:

- Security and Audit Solution – Provides the ability to collect and explore security related data, as well as identify attacks and security breaches.
- Antimalware Assessment Solution – Shows the status of antimalware scans across all servers.
- Activity Log Analytics Solution – Tracks all create, update, and delete activities across all Azure subscriptions.

- Azure Network Security Group Analytics Solution – Provides insight on Azure Network Security Groups.
- Update Management Solution – Identifies and orchestrates installation of missing security updates.

For example, the OMS Security and Audit solution provides forensic analysis, security breech pattern detection, and extensive auditing capabilities. The figure below shows the OMS Security Domain information and Notable Issues. The figure shows that there were 5 malicious traffic events, 9 locked accounts, and 3 password reset attempts, amongst other findings.

This information is invaluable for monitoring the security posture of the organization.

The OMS Threat Intelligence shown in the figure below indicates that there were 18 total threats, all of which were botnet attacks. In addition, it will pinpoint those threats geographically. In the image, there are incoming attacks from North America, Europe, Asia, and Africa.

This kind of detailed information is critical for understanding the nature and origin of the threats facing the organization. The security solutions in Azure OMS provide detailed security collection and analytics.

Operational Monitoring

For operational management, OMS has a number of solutions that provide details operational data collection, analysis, and recommendations. These solutions leverage the huge data repository and knowledge generated by the solution developers to generate insight and advice. The solutions include:

- Active Directory Assessment Solution – Assesses the risk and health of Active Directory.
- Active Directory Replication Status Solution – Identifies replication issues in Active Directory.
- Office 365 Analytics Solution – Gathers data from Office 365 and shows user activity, provides forensics, and allows for audit and compliance.
- SQL Assessment Solution – Assesses the risk and health of SQL.
- Azure SQL Analytics Solution – Azure SQL database monitoring and performance analytics.
- Change Tracking Solution – Collects and tracks changes across the servers including software, registry, file, services, and other key areas.
- Azure Web Apps Analytics Solution – Identify and troubleshoot issues across Azure Web Apps.

- HDInsight HBase Monitoring Solution – Log analytics, monitoring and alerting for Azure HDInsight HBase Linux clusters.

The solutions are designed to require minimal configuration or maintenance, yet delivery detailed insight and recommendations.

For example, the Office 365 Analytics OMS solution has a top-level tile that shows the breakdown of user activity. In the figure below, it's clear that the SharePoint activity is the most common (33.3 thousand activities), OneDrive is next (18.5 thousand activities), and Azure Active Directory least utilized (10 thousand activities).

Drilling in on the Office 365 tile, the dashboard in the figure below shows the detailed breakdown of the activities. For example, it shows that about 50% of all SharePoint Activities are file accesses (16.4 thousand), only 333 files were uploaded, just 83 files were renamed. For the Active Directory, it shows that there were 860 user logins, 281 group updates, and 79 user adds and 10 changed user passwords. For each line in the dashboard, clicking on it will provide a list of the individual records with detailed information.

This information collected, analyzed and presented in the dashboards gives administrators the detailed information they need to make operational decisions and manage the applications.

Performance Metrics

Each solution in OMS collects a wide range of performance metrics and OMS is configured to collect many performance counters by default, including both Windows and Linux. This information can be displayed in many ways in the dashboards. For example, the figure below shows a basic display of processor utilization for Server1 for the past 6 hours.

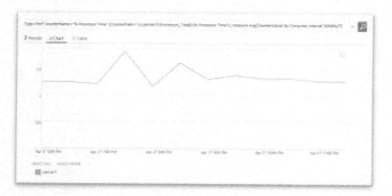

In another example, tiles can be configured to show multiple values with small graphs for visual cues as shown in the figure below.

OMS can even collect and display metrics from external sources. In the figure below, the OMS dashboard is displaying weather data collected and stored in the data repository. The data shows temperature, humidity, and pressure over a 7-day period. Any data can be uploaded to the data repository and then used in analysis and displayed.

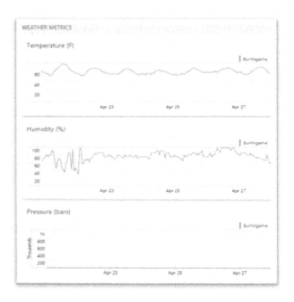

The performance metrics and visualization allow administrators to capture, analyze, and display performance data from a wide variety of sources.

OMS Monitoring the Cloud

Ultimately, Operations Management Suite is a monitoring tool that was born in the Azure cloud, is completed integrated into the Azure cloud, deploys at cloud speed, scales capacity and performance to cloud levels, and evolves at Azure cloud speed, adding features on a weekly basis.

There is no better tool than OMS to monitor the modern hybrid cloud, with its Azure, on-premise, and 3rd party environments.

13 ADDRESSING CLOUD-SCALE NEEDS WITH ON-PREMISE FUNCTIONALITY

The comment frequently comes up, "I like the ability to leverage the cloud, however there are a couple applications we have that we can't move to a public cloud" (because of security, compliance, privacy, reliability reasons). Microsoft's answer to this has been to take their Azure public cloud, and bring the same environment to an on-premise model, that Microsoft calls Azure Stack.

What is Azure Stack?

Azure Stack is effectively Microsoft's Azure cloud brought into an organization's own datacenter. True, under the hood Azure Stack is running Microsoft's Hyper-V, Windows, and Microsoft networking and storage, but you don't see any of that. When you stop and think about it, you are "running Microsoft's Azure in your datacenter!"

It's like saying I'm running an instance of Box.com, or Salesforce.com, or Amazon AWS, or Twitter in my own datacenter. And not just "something that is functionally similar to these cloud offerings," but running Azure Stack is running Microsoft's public Azure cloud in your datacenter!

Running the Public Cloud On-Premise

It would seem counter intuitive to run a public cloud in your own datacenter, however for organizations that have specific security, compliance, and assured reliability expectations that can only be provided "in-house", Azure Stack provides organizations the ability of public cloud technology and "cloud scale" to be run on-premise.

Another reason organizations run public cloud Azure on-premise is to do application compatibility testing, application development, or other testing and development functions on-premise before the application is pushed to a public cloud instance. Azure Stack becomes the intermediary before the application is put in the hosted public cloud environment.

Azure Stack – IaaS, PaaS, and Azure Services

Azure Stack provides operational functions to run virtual machines in an Infrastructure as a Service (IaaS) model, provides Platform as a Service (PaaS) model to run Azure SQL, Azure Web, and MySQL as platform services, as well as provides a range of Azure Services like KeyVault, billing and chargeback functionality, and even Azure Marketplace syndication. As time rolls on, additional services will be included to provide added functional services with Azure public.

Azure Stack for Dev/Test Scenarios

Azure Stack has been a common solution for organizations leveraging Azure for Dev and Test scenarios, however in dual functional methods. One where applications are developed on-premise on Azure Stack, and then hosted in production in Azure (public). And the other where applications are developed in Azure (public) and then hosted on-premise on Azure Stack.

For some organizations, they benefit from an infinitely scalable dev/test environment that Azure (public) provides them, however when it comes to running their application, there might be sensitive or regulated customer or patient data that is best secured within a tightly controlled and managed internal datacenter running Azure Stack.

Other organizations do their development in remote locations where Internet connectivity might not be reliable or of high enough performance to develop in the public Azure cloud, so an Azure Stack on-premise for development provides local connectivity to development resources.

However once the application has been developed and tested, the organization can now push the application up to Azure (public) and leverage the global scale, redundancy, and reliability of the Azure (public) environment.

Azure Stack is being built to provide organizations the ability to completely control the physical location and allocated capacity of their backend environment, and as they develop on the Azure platform, they can then easily shift from a Dev/Test environment (on-premise or public cloud) to a similar Azure environment (on-premise or public cloud) that meets their organizational needs.

Azure Stack for Extremely Secure Environments
Beyond just dev and test scenarios, many organizations need cloud scale, but for security purposes want or need to run the application in-house. Azure (public) has provided a highly reliable and secure platform for organizations, and Azure Stack extends that model to a private highly secured on-premise environment.

Azure Stack for Hosters
Hosters and Managed Service Providers have been leveraging Azure Stack to differentiate their services from other service providers. The world of third party hosted virtual machines has quickly become a commodity as organizations have spun up datacenters, calling themselves "cloud providers," and effectively just hosting virtual machines (Windows and Linux) on traditional hypervisors and platforms (ESXi, Hyper-V, or OpenStack).

But Azure Stack is not a commodity solution that has been "done before," rather as enterprises begin to realize that scalability and agility depend on having a Platform as a Service model in addition to an Infrastructure as a Service model offering. Azure Stack allows hosters to mirror Azure (public) services in specific business areas that has included:
- industry specific Azure Stack hosted models (for healthcare, finance, retail)
- Azure Stack hosted models in region specific areas not served by public cloud providers (like Western Africa, Central America, and the Middle East)
- Azure Stack as a replication datacenter, an addition or alterative to the Microsoft hosted Azure public cloud.

ADDRESSING CLOUD-SCALE NEEDS WITH ON-PREMISE FUNCTIONALITY

ABOUT THE AUTHORS

Chris Amaris, MCITP, MCTS, CISSP: Chris is the chief technology officer and cofounder of Convergent Computing. He has more than 30 years' experience consulting for Fortune 500 companies, leading companies in the technology selection, architecture, design, and deployment of complex enterprise cloud integration projects. Chris specializes in leveraging Microsoft Azure and System Center technologies to achieve high degree of on-premise to cloud integration, migration, automation, and self-service, reducing the level of effort and time-to-market for organizations while providing high levels of fault tolerance and availability.

Marcus Clayton, MCSA, MCSE: Marcus is an accomplished cloud architect, author, and technical enthusiast. He has worked with a wide variety of enterprises modernizing their IT infrastructure, automating business processes and designing cloud strategies. You can keep up with Marcus on his blog automationagenda.com and GitHub contributions github.com/marcusclayton

Rand Morimoto, Ph.D., CISSP, MCSE: Dr Morimoto is the President of Convergent Computing (CCO), a San Francisco Bay Area based strategy and technology consulting firm. CCO helps organizations development and fine tune their technology strategies, and then provide hands-on assistance planning, preparing, implementing, and supporting the technology infrastructures. CCO works with Microsoft and other industry leading hardware and software vendors in early adopter programs, gaining insight and hands-on expertise to the technologies far before they are released to the general public. This early adopter experience has allowed Rand and CCO's experts develop tips, tricks, and best practices based on lessons learned.

Made in the USA
Las Vegas, NV
27 November 2021

35397176R00056